Praise for

*A Dangerous Dozen: Twelve Christians Who
Threatened the Status Quo but Taught Us to Live Like Jesus*

"Surveys the full reach of Christian history and spans the whole globe.... A fine gift—a book that is not only fascinating reading but also a spur to bold and faithful action today."

—Prof. Thomas G. Long, Bandy Professor of Preaching,
Candler School of Theology, Emory University

"Excellent ... reminds us that the gospel is a revolutionary challenge to a world that accepts poverty and war as 'just the way things are.' Holds a mirror up to readers, forcing us to recognize the timid compromises we make in order to feel secure and prosperous. The way of Jesus, as Robertson makes clear, is far more challenging—and rewarding!"

—Michael Kinnamon, general secretary,
National Council of Churches

"An antidote to individualistic piety and the assumption that Christianity is inherently conservative.... A much-needed challenge to transform our safe faith into a dangerous, powerful force for good."

—Dr. James F. McGrath, Clarence L. Goodwin
Chair in New Testament Language and Literature,
Department of Philosophy and Religion, Butler University

"Robertson gives us a dozen stirring exemplars who have challenged the world's conventional wisdom on behalf of the gospel. Read and learn, and discover your own courage to love as God loves."

—The Most Rev. Katharine Jefferts Schori,
presiding bishop of The Episcopal Church; author,
The Heartbeat of God: Finding the Sacred in the Middle of Everything

"Engaging and refreshing ... lifts up special people who model faith in life. Anyone looking to apply Christian faith to the challenges of today will be guided by the stories of these twelve courageous servants of God."

—The Rev. Donald J. McCoid, Ecumenical and Inter-Religious
Relations, Evangelical Lutheran Church in America

"The full force of exemplary lives can be lost on us so easily without the kind of fresh, contemporary portraits we find here. Robertson makes the compelling witness of these saints burn bright in our world."

—Prof. Jon Nilson, Loyola University;
former president, Catholic Theological Society of America

"Invites us all to listen to that inner voice that continues to call us all—as ordinary people—to stand up and do extraordinary things for God."

—Fr. Albert Cutié, radio/TV host;
author, *Dilemma: A Priest's Struggle with Faith and Love*

"One need not be a Christian to appreciate that those who inspire are to be cherished wherever and however they manifest.... [A] welcome balm at a time when the world too often seems devoid of true spiritual leadership."

—Ira Rifkin, editor, *Spiritual Leaders Who Changed the World:
The Essential Handbook to the Past Century of Religion*

"One part Bible study, several parts history lesson, 100 percent good storytelling ... provide[s] us a fresh look at folks we thought we knew and introduce[s] us to people we ought to meet—exemplary women and men from many centuries and almost every continent, together reminding us of the breadth of Christian activism."

—Dr. Lucinda Mosher, Senior Fellow, Auburn
Theological Seminary; author, *Faith in the Neighborhood*

"Celebrates the lives of twelve heroes who dared to step into darkness bearing the light of God's love, no matter what the cost. These tales of danger, risk and sacrifice for Jesus's sake are indeed inspiring."

—Michael Rhodes, five-time Emmy award–winning
filmmaker; president, Film Clips, Inc.

"A clear and vivid picture of twelve men and women who would not stand still when the world needed to be pushed, or remain silent when power needed to be challenged. My hope is that the questions for reflection at the end of each chapter will help us to rethink our ministry in the service of God's mission in our own time."

—Archbishop Fred Hiltz, primate, The Anglican Church of Canada

"Clear and very pleasing prose, with a sure and sympathetic command of his subjects, a *Lives of the Saints* for our times. [This] 'dangerous dozen' and their escapades of faith ... will instruct and encourage certainly; but beware, for they will also inevitably seduce and charm you as well."

—Phyllis Tickle, popular speaker;
author, *The Great Emergence* and *The Words of Jesus*

12 Christians
Who
Threatened
the
Status
Quo

A DANGeRoUS Dozen

but
Taught
Us
to Live
Like
Jesus

The Rev. Canon
C. K. ROBERTSON, PhD
Foreword by
Archbishop DESMOND TUTU

Walking Together, Finding the Way ®
SKYLIGHT PATHS®
PUBLISHING
Woodstock, Vermont

A Dangerous Dozen:
12 Christians Who Threatened the Status Quo but Taught Us to Live Like Jesus

2011 Quality Paperback Edition, First Printing
© 2011 by C. K. Robertson
Foreword © 2011 by Desmond Tutu

Library of Congress Cataloging-in-Publication Data
Robertson, C. K. (Charles Kevin), 1964–
A dangerous dozen : 12 Christians who threatened the status quo but taught us to live like Jesus / C. K. Robertson ; foreword by Desmond Tutu.—Quality pbk. ed.
p. cm.
Includes bibliographical references.
ISBN 978-1-59473-298-0 (quality pbk. original) 1. Christian biography. 2. Church history. 3. Change—Religious aspects—Christianity. 4. Christian leadership. I. Title. II. Title: 12 Christians who threatened the status quo but taught us to live like Jesus. III. Title: Twelve Christians who threatened the status quo but taught us to live like Jesus.
BR1700.3.R63 2011
270.092'2—dc22

2011000667

10 9 8 7 6 5 4 3 2 1
Manufactured in the United States of America

Cover Design: Jenny Buono
Text Design: Kristi Menter

SkyLight Paths is creating a place where people of different spiritual traditions come together for challenge and inspiration, a place where we can help each other understand the mystery that lies at the heart of our existence.

SkyLight Paths sees both believers and seekers as a community that increasingly transcends traditional boundaries of religion and denomination—people wanting to learn from each other, walking together, finding the way.

SkyLight Paths, "Walking Together, Finding the Way," and colophon are trademarks of LongHill Partners, Inc., registered in the U.S. Patent and Trademark Office.

Walking Together, Finding the Way®
Published by SkyLight Paths Publishing
A Division of LongHill Partners, Inc.
Sunset Farm Offices, Route 4, P.O. Box 237
Woodstock, VT 05091
Tel: (802) 457-4000 Fax: (802) 457-4004
www.skylightpaths.com

To Michael Rhodes,
five-time Emmy award–winning filmmaker,
founder of Film Clips, Inc., and dear friend,
with thanks for introducing me to some
of these "dangerous" characters.

Contents

Foreword by Archbishop Desmond Tutu   ix

Acknowledgments   xi

Prologue: The Outlaw   xiii

1 **Paul of Tarsus:** The Catalyst   1

2 **Mary Magdalene:** The Witness   17

3 **Origen of Alexandria:** The Innovator   31

4 **Francis of Assisi:** The Radical   45

5 **Hildegard of Bingen:** The Visionary   59

6 **Thomas Cranmer:** The Reformer   72

7 **Sojourner Truth:** The Liberator   85

8 **Dorothy Day:** The Activist   95

9 **Dietrich Bonhoeffer:** The Resister   107

10 **Janani Luwum:** The Revivalist   121

11 **Oscar Romero:** The Advocate   133

12 **K. H. Ting:** The Reconstructionist   146

Epilogue   162

Notes   166

Foreword

This newest book by Chuck Robertson examines the lives of courageous people who were not always appreciated or even understood when they stood up in the name of Jesus against injustice. The Church has a call to prophetic ministry, but the way of the prophet is often hard. But each of the individuals in these pages was willing to challenge the structures of society and the Church, even on their own when no one else would join them.

In South Africa, I think immediately of that great witness (*martus*, or martyr) for our Lord, Dr. Beyers Naude. He was a pastor of the white Dutch Reformed Church, to which most Afrikaners and therefore the apartheid government belonged. This denomination provided that government with a theological justification for the racial injustice of apartheid. For a long time, Naude had gone along with this view. In 1960, the Sharpeville massacre happened, when white police fired on a peaceful demonstration against the pass laws, which severely restricted the movements of blacks. There was an international outcry, and the World Council of Churches convened the Cottesloe Consultation to discuss the fraught situation with South African member churches, which included the white Dutch Reformed Church. This conference resolved that there was no biblical basis for apartheid. The government of Dr. Hendrik Verwoerd, the prime minister, was livid. He insisted that the delegation of the Dutch Reformed Church should repudiate the Cottesloe Declaration. That Church succumbed meekly and even suspended its membership in the World Council of Churches. But not everyone in that delegation meekly succumbed. Dr. Naude stood by the conference and was forced to resign as minister of a very prominent congregation. He left to join the black Dutch Reformed Church, something unheard in race-obsessed South Africa. He was placed under a strict banning order, a form of house arrest, for seven years. He was ostracized and vilified. But he lived to see freedom come in South Africa, when he was vindicated wonderfully. The General Synod of the white Dutch Reformed Church apologized publicly to him and to others of its members who had been repudiated and vilified. When he died, Beyers Naude was buried from the church from which he had been forced to resign.

Times change and situations seem to change, but there is still a great need for prophets, for God's ambassadors, to stand up and be counted. Who will dare to be Paul the Apostle today, or Dorothy Day, or Francis of Assisi, or Dietrich Bonhoeffer? Who will dare, when God calls, to say, "Here I am, Lord, send me"?

The Right Reverend Desmond Tutu
Archbishop Emeritus of Southern Africa and Nobel Laureate

Acknowledgments

What a delight it has been to discover such enthusiastic teammates, coaches, and cheerleaders at SkyLight Paths. Special appreciation goes to Emily Wichland, who was always ready to listen to my questions and find the answers together. And what a pleasure it has been to work once more with Nancy Fitzgerald, my editor on a previous book. Now, as then, she offered needed encouragement and sage advice.

I am indebted to Desmond Tutu for agreeing in his retirement to "make an exception" and contribute the foreword to this book. Truly he is one of my greatest heroes and an inspiration for this work. Thank you, Arch!

During the writing of this book, I said final goodbyes to my father, Francis E. Robertson, devoted husband of fifty-six years, father of five, grandfather of four, retired U.S. Army colonel, long-time NASA employee ... and faithful Christian. Remembering him and my mother, Virginia M. Robertson, who died over a decade before, I am reminded yet again of the blessing of family. I only hope that I will pass on to my own children even a fraction of all that I have received.

PROLOGUE

The Outlaw

In one of the most notable movies about World War II, a ragtag group of undesirables is recruited to undertake a suicide mission behind enemy lines on the eve of D-Day. In exchange for infiltrating the German headquarters and killing key commanders, these recruits are promised a full pardon if they should survive—an unlikely prospect.

These men were called the "dirty dozen," charged with a heroic and almost impossible task. Their superiors preferred to see them disappear after the mission than to have to deal with them later. They were necessary ... but dangerous.

The twelve dangerous people included in this book weren't criminals, but sometimes they were seen as undesirables, too. In their respective times they often were viewed as somehow odd, out of sync with the world around them. In the earliest years of Christianity, the apostle Paul declared that God had chosen "the foolish in the world to shame the wise" (1 Corinthians 1:27). St. Francis of Assisi spoke happily of being a "fool for Christ,"[1] and Peter Maurin, mentor to Dorothy Day, recited in verse, "They say that I am crazy, because I refuse to be crazy the way everyone else is crazy."[2]

They were Christian change agents, unafraid to ask what God would have them do in the face of life's realities—and unafraid to

xiii

go ahead and do it. Instead of simply wearing a "What Would Jesus Do?" bracelet or T-shirt, they chose serious engagement in the name of Jesus with the hurts and injustices of their world. The Church needed them—but didn't necessarily *want* them. They were in good company, though: Jesus of Nazareth, in whose name they served, was considered a little crazy by his own family and seen as a big threat by both the political and religious leaders of his time.

A DANGEROUS MAN

In *The Brothers Karamazov*, Russian novelist Fyodor Dostoyevsky muses that if Jesus had returned to earth in his time, he would have posed a threat to the Church bearing his name.[3] The book's story-within-a-story, "The Grand Inquisitor," has Jesus return to fifteenth-century Spain during the time of the Inquisition, when so many Christians were coerced under torture to prove themselves faithful.

When Jesus shows up unexpectedly, he's arrested by religious authorities and imprisoned for causing trouble. The Grand Inquisitor explains to Jesus that he cannot be allowed to roam free, for he might upset the system of power and control that the Church has constructed over the millennia. What Jesus has to offer—what the Inquisitor fears most—is the reminder to the masses that they have the gift of free will. If they realize that, the Inquisitor says, anarchy would ensue. Couldn't Jesus see that it was fine for him to be worshipped, but simply unacceptable for him to be emulated?

From the Grand Inquisitor's perspective, it's an issue of stability and order. Systems, of course—then as now—move toward stability and equilibrium. Consider, for example, an airplane's navigational system. The plane does not fly in a perfectly straight line from point A to point B, but allows for slight variations along the route. It doesn't change its course, but those small course corrections prevent major, substantial change. A thermostat, too, allows for small variations in order to return repeatedly to the desired temperature. These are self-regulating patterns that maintain the status quo of the overall system.

In much the same way, human beings set up social systems to help them regulate an otherwise fearful and fragile existence. The ancient world offered people little control over life, death, and their environment. Finding meaning in the will of the gods or in the divine order of the universe offered a sense of well-being and hope.

During Jesus's lifetime, he and his fellow Palestinian Jews found themselves in a precarious position, under the control of the Roman conquerors, who set up camp in the very shadow of the Temple. It is easy to understand why the Jewish leaders of that time placed great emphasis on religious regulations and rites and on the boundaries between insiders and outsiders. Directives about what and with whom you could eat, and with whom and in what way you could have sexual relations, allowed the community to live with a degree of confidence in an otherwise fragile existence. For people who were no longer masters of their own destiny, a religious system of clear rules and boundaries created a place of safety and stability.

The Romans were in a delicate situation, too. Though they were masters of the known world, in Palestine they were on the edge of the empire, in a place where they did not understand the religious customs, much less the zeal, of the resident monotheists. The *Pax Romana*—the Roman Peace—was set up to allow a sense of peace for conqueror and conquered alike. Local control was allowed in order to maintain control on the larger level.

To all those who sought some measure of control, then, Jesus was a dangerous man who questioned the authority of both political and religious leaders. In the 1970s, singer-songwriter Larry Norman wrote "The Outlaw," which depicts Jesus as a man who befriended "unschooled ruffians," "spoke out against corruption," xvi Prologue: The Outlaw

and "bowed to no decree." In the end, Norman sings, the religious and political leaders "feared his strength and power" and were complicit in arranging his death. The same characteristics that caused these leaders' concerns in Jesus's own time would likewise cause concern in subsequent centuries—in the Spanish Inquisition and in our own day and throughout the millennia—for leaders of the Church that Jesus founded.

GOSPEL TRUTH

Opposition to Jesus is a theme in all four Gospels of the Christian scriptures. In each of them we can see the dangers Jesus posed to the establishment—and to the opposition that seemed to rise up against him wherever he went.

Mark

In Mark, the first narrative of Jesus's life to be written, opposition to Jesus appears almost as soon as he begins his ministry. After healing a paralytic, Jesus declares that the man's sins are forgiven. Immediately, "some of the scribes were sitting there, questioning in their hearts" how Jesus could dare to say such a thing (Mark 2:6). To them, he is a blasphemer (2:7). To them, Jesus seems to flaunt a kind of lawless freedom. A little later, they are shocked and irritated when Jesus eats with tax collectors and those considered "sinners" (2:16) and when his disciples ignore the rules for fasting on the Sabbath (2:18 and 2:24). And by Mark's third chapter, the religious authorities—the scribes and Pharisees—actively conspire against him (3:6), and his own family members, hearing that he's lost his mind (3:21), seek to restrain him. Throughout Mark's Gospel, whether condemned as a blasphemer or derided as a madman, Jesus is in trouble for his apparent disregard for the religious laws that the institutional leaders hold sacrosanct. When he finally arrives in Jerusalem from the countryside, the chief priests and elders challenge his bold reinterpretation of regulations: "By what authority are you doing these things? Who gave you this authority to do them?" (11:28). As often is the case in Mark's Gospel, Jesus answers their question with another question, putting them on the spot and calling their own authority into question. The crowds know it, and that makes the religious leaders all the more hostile.

Matthew

The Gospel of Matthew—which appears first in the Christian scriptures—divides the teachings of Jesus into five large blocks of material, in much the same way that the Five Books of Moses, which make up the Torah, contain the Jewish Law. Indeed, Matthew seems to go out of his way to show how Jesus, on the deepest level, fulfills the Mosaic Law, in contrast to the claims of his opponents. If Jesus poses a threat in Matthew's Gospel, it is not that he lets people off the hook, but rather that he sets a higher standard. Chapters 5–7 open the first block of teachings that insist, "You have heard it said ... but I say...." This verbal formula becomes Jesus's familiar refrain, as he reminds his listeners that it's not enough to follow the rules and regulations with which the authorities are so familiar and comfortable. The parables in Matthew instead emphasize mercy and compassion over legalistic adherence to specific regulations and again and again point out that Jesus's religious contemporaries are hypocrites. "The scribes and the Pharisees sit in Moses's seat," Jesus insists; "therefore, do whatever they teach you and follow it; but do not do as they do, for they do not practice what they teach" (Matthew 23:2–3). These are fighting words: Jesus in Matthew's Gospel sets himself at odds with the religious leaders of his time. The final parable (25:31–46) speaks of the judgment of the nations in terms of how they show, or fail to show, compassion to the poor and the marginalized— "the least of these." Compassion, Jesus asserts, both fulfills the Law and trumps it.

Luke

In the Gospel of Luke, Jesus incurs the hostility of the authorities not as much in response to his approach to the religious laws but for his openness to outsiders. In this Gospel, Jesus inaugurates his ministry in his hometown synagogue, reading from the prophet Isaiah: "The Spirit of the Lord God is upon me ..." (Isaiah 61:1). The words that follow in this scriptural passage clearly link the proclamation of good news with acts of power and liberation (Luke 4:18). When Jesus finishes reading, he declares to the congregation that he himself is the fulfillment of Isaiah's prophecy, the much-anticipated "servant of the Lord," the ambassador sent by God. This in itself is noteworthy, as the Greek word for "sent," *apostelō*, is at the root of the word "apostle." An apostle is a "sent one," and in Luke's Gospel, Jesus is the prototype, the model of an apostle sent by God.

As the congregation listens in astonishment, Jesus expands the definition of the kind of people to whom God's apostles are sent (Luke 4:26–29). By referencing Elijah's ministry to the widow of Zarephath in Sidon and Elisha's healing of Naaman the Syrian—both outsiders to Israel—Jesus declares that God's "sent ones" are sent to outsiders as well as to insiders. The story ends with a literal cliff-hanger: the residents of Jesus's hometown, "filled with rage" (4:28) try to hurl Jesus off a cliff, but he moves calmly through their midst and disappears.

Throughout Luke's Gospel, Jesus's apostolic ministry involves reaching out to the marginal groups of his time, those deemed unsuitable or inferior. As in Mark and Matthew, there are debates between Jesus and the Pharisees about infringements of the Mosaic Law, but it is the obvious and intentional focus on outsiders that makes Luke's Gospel stand out. Women and children, servants and slaves, Samaritans and Romans, all those considered to be "sinners"—all are welcomed by Jesus. Even the parables in Luke's Gospel turn the stereotypes of Jesus's world upside down: the

Prodigal Son, for example, celebrates a father's radical love for his undeserving, degenerate son (Luke 15:11–32). The most astonishing parable, though, is that of the Good Samaritan (10:25–37), an oxymoron to any of Jesus's hearers or Luke's readers. Here, a priest and a Levite, well-respected members of the religious establishment, show no mercy for a stranger robbed and left for dead. The unlikely hero of the story is a Samaritan—a member of a group despised by Jews—whose genuine compassion is presented as a model of godly behavior. To those religious leaders who believed Samaritans to be beneath contempt, this was simply too much to swallow.

Luke also records the appointment of an additional group of "sent ones" besides the twelve apostles, seventy others who are sent ahead of Jesus to prepare the way and minister to the poor and sick (Luke 10:1). In reaching out to—and even making heroes of—those generally avoided by his religious contemporaries, Jesus proves himself to be a threat to an establishment that prizes clear boundaries between the insiders and the outsiders.

John

The Gospel according to John takes a different approach from the other three Gospels, raising the level of opposition and offering a different motivation for it. While Mark, Matthew, and Luke all depict Jesus casting out the money changers in the Temple during the final week of his life, John places the story at the very beginning of Jesus's ministry (John 2). And in this Gospel, the intense opposition Jesus faces comes not from the infringement of religious regulations or the breaking down of social barriers between insiders and outsiders. Here, the catalyst for the hostility is Jesus's statements about himself. The so-called "I am" speeches of Jesus in John—marking his self-definition as the way, the truth, the life, the bread of life, the door, the good shepherd, the resurrection and life, the light of the world—incur the wrath of the religious leaders, the crowds, even his siblings. In a climactic moment, when his enemies accuse Jesus of trying to make himself out to be superior to Abraham, the father of the Jewish faith, his answer is immediate and provocative: "Before Abraham was, I AM" (John 8:58). In the Hebrew scriptures, "I AM" is the very name of the Divine. That makes Jesus's declaration a threat to the core of the religious system. It's little wonder, then, that his listeners immediately try to stone him as a blasphemer (8:59). Although they offer different reasons for the opposition Jesus faced, all four Gospels agree that he faced strong antagonism, that it came from the religious establishment, and that it resulted from the perception of Jesus as a threat to that establishment. Jesus was the prototypical "sent one," but he seemed to be sent not to stabilize the religious system but to upset it. The weary masses who had endured countless burdens placed on them by their religious leaders flocked to him by the thousands. The "sinners" who could never do enough to overcome the stigma that clung to them sought him out and embraced him. The seekers who looked in his eyes and saw something more, something deeper, left everything and followed him.

BLESSED ARE THE TROUBLEMAKERS

Down through the centuries, followers of this troublesome Jesus have been causing trouble themselves in countless ways. This book recounts the stories of twelve of them—a dangerous dozen. Had they stayed to themselves and chosen the way of the hermit, they might have engendered nothing more than bemused curiosity. But their words and actions challenged the status quo, and they—like the Jesus they sought to follow—were viewed as threats by the religious establishment of their own times. In the Middle Ages, at the height of the Church's power, wealth, and influence, a curious little man from Italy's Umbrian hills called on people to give all their possessions away and live simple lives in the name of Jesus. A former persecutor of the Church challenged the empire and brought the good news of Jesus all over the known world and helped define Christianity forever. A would-be military hero pointed the way to true peacemaking. A quiet bookworm helped people see what true courage means. It has been through the words and actions of surprising individuals like these that the face of Jesus has been shown to the Church and the world.

At times the actions of these individuals resulted in hostile reaction by the system. At other times, the response was a more subtle policy of "canonize and control." If you can't kill them, the authorities seemed to reason, then manage them. Put them on a pedestal and make them appear so otherworldly that they become irrelevant. It is little wonder that American social activist Dorothy Day once declared, "Don't call me a saint. I don't want to be dismissed that easily." Whether they were killed or simply killed with kindness, these blessed troublemakers followed Jesus no matter what—and paid a price for it. This is no surprise, for, as Dietrich Bonhoeffer, the German Lutheran pastor and theologian who opposed the Nazi regime, reminds us, there is always a cost to discipleship.

We who say we will follow Jesus would do well to remember that. The dangerous dozen Christians in this book never forgot it.

For Reflection

1. Some people say that being a "good Christian" is primarily about believing the right things about Jesus. Others say that it is primarily about living like Jesus and following his principles. What do you think ... and why?

2. Jesus has been depicted in different ways at different times, in books, movies, advertising. What depiction of Jesus most closely resonates with you? Are there any that you don't like or don't appreciate? Why?

3. If someone asked you who Jesus is to you, what would be your answer?

For Further Reading

Borg, Marcus J. *Jesus: Uncovering the Life, Teachings, and Relevance of a Religious Revolutionary.* New York: HarperOne, 2008.

Burridge, Richard. *Four Gospels, One Jesus: A Symbolic Reading.* 2nd ed. Grand Rapids: Eerdmans, 2005.

Miller, Robert J., ed. *The Complete Gospels.* 4th ed. Salem, OR: Polebridge Press, 2010.

Niebuhr, Richard H. *Christ and Culture.* New York: Harper, 1956.

Wright, N. T. *Who Was Jesus?* Grand Rapids: Eerdmans, 1993.

PAUL OF TARSUS

The Catalyst

He would become the chief architect of Christianity and, indeed, one of the most famous individuals in the history of the world. But when we first encounter Paul of Tarsus in the Acts of the Apostles, he is simply a young man present at the stoning of Stephen, a controversial follower of Jesus of Nazareth. But Paul was no neutral spectator at the deadly event. Fully approving of Stephen's death, Paul held the cloaks of the executioners, freeing their hands to grab more stones.

Yet it was only a short while later that this same Paul would become the Christian faith's most ardent propagator—and its biggest troublemaker. For this same person who went on to plant churches also seeded them with ideas of equality and mutuality, at least within the Church system. Paul moved 180 degrees, from being an opponent to change to an apostle of change.

1

A MAN OF TWO WORLDS

What do we know of Paul's pre-Christian life? The book of Acts, in the Christian scriptures, says that that he studied at the feet of Gamaliel, a leading first-century rabbi, noted for his wisdom and tolerance, who called for a moderate response on the part of the Jerusalem religious leaders toward Peter and the other apostles, arguing that this new movement would probably die out on its own. But if it was of divine origin, he warned, those who opposed it may be fighting against God. It was under such an astute mentor that Paul studied, and he soon became a rising rabbinic scholar in his own right. From his own letters, we learn that Paul advanced beyond many of his peers largely because of his zeal for the traditions of his ancestors. He was proud of his ancestry and his faith. Paul, also known by his Hebrew name, Saul, was a descendent of the tribe of Benjamin, as was his ancient namesake, Israel's first king. Although a "Hebrew of Hebrews," Paul was also intensely proud of his Roman citizenship and was well versed in the poetry and philosophy of the Greek and Roman world. Whether it was the result of meritorious service done by his parents or some other reason, Paul was born a Roman citizen, a rare honor for one of the occupied peoples in Palestine. He was, in truth, a man of two worlds, with an impressive pedigree in each. So what was this potential star doing chasing down a motley crew of sectarians, especially when his own mentor advised a more lenient course?

Like a good mystery story, the answer just might be hiding in plain sight. Gamaliel had encountered disciples like Peter and John, who showed every sign of being both faithful to their Jewish heritage and respectful of surrounding Roman customs and laws. Paul faced a different kind of follower in the more radical Stephen. To Peter and his colleagues, Jesus was the one who would one day restore the kingdom to Israel, so they had little reason to move beyond the shadow of the Temple or provoke their Roman occupiers. To Stephen, on the other hand, Jesus changed everything, making the Temple—and all that it represented in terms of the religious and social boundaries between Jews and Gentiles—irrelevant. There is an irony here. Paul was in his own self a man of two worlds, at once the Roman Paulus and the Hebrew Saul, yet he kept these worlds separate and distinct. The danger to Paul in Stephen's message was a blurring of important boundaries on which ancient Israel's very existence depended. For this reason, Paul set out on the road from Jerusalem to Damascus to try to bring an end to what he saw as a dangerous movement—only to face what he dreaded most.

"Saul, Saul, why do you persecute me?" With a blinding light and a fall to the ground, Paul heard the heavenly voice. "Who are you, Lord?" he asked, only to hear the answer he did not want to hear: "I am Jesus, whom you are persecuting" (Acts 9:3–5). As he would often remind both friends and opponents alike in later years, Paul's encounter with Jesus was no less real, no less authentic than Peter's or any of the other apostles. He may not have walked with Jesus for three years as they did, but he met him on the road to Damascus and was forever changed as a result. Blinded by the experience and led by the hand into the city, for three days Paul was buried in darkness, until he was baptized by a disciple named Ananias and had his eyes opened to a whole new life. The former persecutor of the faith now became its greatest proponent. The road *from* Damascus would take him far beyond the social and religious boundaries he once guarded, leading him—and his radical message—to the ends of the earth.

ONE IN JESUS

From the moment of his conversion, Paul faced opposition from within. At first it was his former life that frightened the apostles. After all, everyone knew that he had tried to arrest and even kill followers of Jesus. It took one of the apostles' biggest benefactors, Barnabas—the "son of encouragement"—to vouch for Paul and secure a reluctant seal of approval from the apostles. Indeed,

Barnabas did more than stand up for Paul; he also took Paul with him as his protégé when he left Jerusalem for the Syrian city of Antioch, where together they helped nurture a different kind of Christian community.

It was what Paul learned from this experience and then replicated in many other places that made the apostles—and a lot of other people both inside and outside the Church—even more nervous about him. For at the heart of Paul's message was a complete breakdown of all the boundaries and social divisions that he himself had previously guarded. He put it succinctly in a letter to the Christians in Galatia: "There is neither Jew nor Greek, male nor female, slave nor free, but all are one in Christ" (Galatians 3:28).

It is almost impossible now to appreciate how radical a message this was to those who lived in the Mediterranean world of the first century. Our much-vaunted modern notion of individualism would have been incomprehensible to those who understood themselves as parts of a larger whole or, more likely, several larger wholes. As one ancient Roman once wrote, "That which is not in the interests of the hive cannot be in the interests of the bee."[1] Belonging was what gave someone an identity and purpose. First-century people lived their lives in a series of relational networks. Some were formal networks, like voluntary associations, clubs, and trade guilds. Some were based on political and religious ties. Still others were more informal, like those connections between patrons and clients, masters and servants. We have already seen that Paul was a man of two worlds, which meant that he could move in and out of synagogues on the one hand, but on the other hand he had invested enough in his Roman side that he understood his rights as a citizen. Plus, he was a "tent maker" or, more generally, a leatherworker, which means that he either belonged to a trade guild or at least knew his way around the informal networks of leatherworkers, so that he was able to find some fellow craftsmen when he came into a new city.

Yet, with his message that "all are one in Christ," Paul set up a new possibility: a network that demanded primary allegiance from its members and in which all other distinctions between people became secondary or even irrelevant. As he went from city to city, organizing groups of believers, Paul did four things that would have lasting ramifications for the Christian movement.

First, he had them meet in homes—what we now call "house churches"—instead of more official building sites. Paul sought out fairly well-off persons with homes big enough to hold a group because he appreciated the importance of the intimacy that comes from a member's home.

Second, Paul adapted a nonreligious word, *ecclesia*, to refer to the groups he formed. The word would be translated into English as "church," but it was a political term when Paul first appropriated it. It referred to the gathering of free citizens of a city, peers who were equal under the law. He did not use the Jewish term "synagogue" or *cultus*—which was used for the Greek and Roman religions—to describe this new community, but rather a term that was both recognizable and inviting, especially to those who could never hope to be part of the secular *ecclesia*, but who could hold their heads high in the house church of God's *ecclesia*.

Third, Paul used family terminology to describe the relationships within that community. Like some other fraternal organizations in his time, he was not shy about addressing his fellow members as "brothers" and "sisters," but unlike the secular groups, Paul grounded his sibling language in the reality of their common adoption in Jesus. Whatever their relationships outside the household of faith—master and slave, patron and client—within it these members were to view themselves and one another as beloved siblings.

Finally, Paul underscored this emphasis on valuing one another by using the metaphor of the "Body of Christ" to describe the life of the Christian community. The body analogy had been used by others, but while secular philosophers focused on the organizational unity represented by the human body, Paul impressed upon the community the importance of their diversity as well. It wasn't just the wealthy and highborn who had something to offer the group. Even the seemingly insignificant member was to be respected and honored.

All this brings us back to Paul's formula—"neither Jew nor Greek, male nor female, slave nor free"—and the opposition it provoked. His idea that the Christian community had primacy of place among all other relational networks meant, in practical terms, that members should let go of the old distinctions and identity markers of the surrounding world. Now Paul was no social activist. He didn't fight for equal rights outside the Christian system. His focus was wholly and completely within the community of believers. There, Paul was clear that you couldn't have it both ways; you could not speak of equality in Jesus and at the same time act as if you were superior to one another. To those who were on the bottom tiers of first-century society, Paul's words meant liberation. To those at the top, though, who had a stake in keeping the relational structures of the outside world in place, Paul's message was a challenge, one they intended to answer.

BATTLE WON?

Things came to a head early on in Paul's ministry, as fellow Jewish believers in Jesus, like himself, confronted what appeared to them to be his over-lenient policy of welcoming non-Jews into the community without demanding that they also be circumcised. Their reasoning made sense, for they understood that circumcision was the gateway to a life lived in obedience to the Law of Moses, the collection of regulations that helped an entire people survive intact throughout centuries of wars, exile, and foreign oversight. What Paul seemed to advocate was a breakdown of barriers between Jew and non-Jew that could essentially lead to the loss of Jewish identity through total assimilation, something that the pre-converted Paul himself had sought to prevent.

The uproar was enough that a council of leaders was convened in Jerusalem, where the Christian movement first began. Overseen by James, the brother of Jesus and head of the church in that city, the council adopted a compromise that was deemed acceptable by all. Gentiles were to be accepted into the community without undergoing circumcision, but at the same time they were to be given a short list of restrictions regarding areas where there was particular danger of cultural assimilation and loss of identity. Both newcomers and insiders were asked to make concessions for the sake of the other. But it didn't work out quite that easily.

Problems arose on both sides. Traditionalists like Peter, chief among the twelve apostles, went back and forth over full acceptance of non-Jewish members, even refusing to be seen at the dinner table with them on one occasion, when ambassadors from James showed up in the area. Plus, the worst fears of Paul's opponents were realized in places like Corinth, the "sin city" of its day, as church members fell into the more immoral patterns of the surrounding culture. Whether through pleading or haranguing, Paul fought an uphill battle on two fronts, crying out for the full inclusion of uncircumcised members without circumcising them even as he sought to instill discipline and respect within the group based on love instead of legalism. His priority, as seen in every letter he wrote to the various churches, was the promotion of unity between the Jews and non-Jews in Jesus.

In one sense, he won the battle. In the end, Gentiles were indeed welcomed and recognized as full members, without being required to take a next step beyond baptism. Of course, this may have had as much to do with the changing demographics in membership as with Paul's leadership. Even with the impressive growth of the group in Jerusalem on Pentecost—shortly after Jesus's earthly ministry—when three thousand were added to their number, in terms of the overall population of the empire, numbers and influence were on the side of the Gentiles. In fact, by the end of his life, in his Letter to the Romans, Paul found himself advocating for the Jewish members of his churches, begging the now non-Jewish majority not to forget that their Jewish brothers and sisters constituted the vine onto which Gentiles were later grafted. Paul may have "won" the battle for Gentiles' inclusion, but this didn't mean that he realized his dream of mutual respect and unity between Jew and non-Jew. In fact, even as he fought to the end for love over all, the seeds of anti-Semitism were taking root and developing within churches.

TURNING THE WORLD UPSIDE DOWN

Recalling the other two dichotomies in Paul's formula, "male and female, slave and free," the apostle most certainly did not win the day—but it wasn't for lack of trying. From early in his work, Paul saw the value of including women in his leadership team. In a time when wives were unnamed helpers in the shadow of their husbands, he counted among his closest teammates Priscilla and Aquila—even naming Priscilla, the wife, first, presumably because of her gifts and skills. Phoebe and Lydia were other significant players in the early days of the Christian movement, and by the time he wrote one of his last letters, the Epistle to the Romans, Paul listed an entire chapter's worth of colleagues—and almost half were women! One was even described as an apostle or considered highly by the apostles (Romans 16:7; it is not clear how to read the sentence), an amazing statement about her leadership skills. Paul seemed to take seriously his own formula and made a point of empowering gifted women for service right alongside men.

As for the issue of slavery, he took a more personal approach. When in prison himself, Paul encountered a runaway slave named Onesimus, whose Latin name means "useless." Seeing the passion and gifts in this individual, Paul nurtured him as a brother and leader in Jesus. And when the time came for Onesimus to be released, Paul wrote a brief but powerful letter to Philemon, the former slave's master and host of a house church, arguing that Onesimus had through his conversion become very useful indeed to Paul and could be so to Philemon and others in the church—as a brother and not as a slave. And they were indeed brothers in Jesus. After all, as Paul not so subtly wrote, Philemon, like Onesimus, had come to faith in Jesus through Paul, which made Paul a loving parent to them both. In the end, it was love that Paul was trying to instill in Philemon toward Onesimus, for the latter had become so dear to Paul and could be to Philemon as well. The Letter to Philemon is an intensely personal plea about a particular situation, yet the circumstances were far from unique in first-century society and, thus, in first-century churches. For this reason, Paul's personal plea to Philemon could serve as a template for other master-slave situations.

In the book of Acts, Paul and his companions were said by his opponents to have "turned the world upside down" (Acts 17:6). This was not empty hyperbole. By empowering women and arguing for the equality of former slaves, Paul was indeed turning the ways of the first-century world on their head. It was one thing to open the doorway to Gentile converts, for this would only upset the delicate balance of one small subset of the vast empire. But these other things were more serious.

It is little surprise, then, that when opposition came, it came in the form of personal attacks, attempts to discredit Paul as an apostle. His enemies loudly maintained that he could not be an apostle because there already were twelve apostles, a perfect number for matching the pattern of twelve tribes and twelve patriarchs of the ancient Hebrew scriptures. There was no room for a "baker's dozen." More than this, each of the twelve apostles had accompanied Jesus during his three-year ministry. Paul could call himself whatever he wanted, his opponents contended, but he could not legitimately claim to be an apostle of Jesus, since he had never even met him. Paul spent a lot of time in several letters defending his own apostleship, explaining that although he may not have walked with Jesus in Palestine before the crucifixion, he certainly met the resurrected Jesus on the Damascus Road. He proclaimed that his apostolic appointment was nothing less than divine, and he would not take a backseat to those in leadership in Jerusalem, even the twelve. As time went on, the apostleship question raised its head again and again. But because he had personally established so many churches in so many places, because he had "fathered" so many Christians, because he had written so many letters that promoted his positions, it was not possible to completely dishonor Paul ... at least while he was alive.

DOMESTICATING PAUL

Paul's body was hardly in its grave when some church leaders began to revise his more controversial views, especially those concerning women. In Paul's first letter to the Christians in Corinth, two notable sections deal with women, placing strong restrictions on them. The more well-known is the following:

> As in all the churches of the saints, women should be silent in the churches. For they are not permitted to speak, but should be subordinate, as the law also says. If there is anything they desire to know, let them ask their husbands at home. For it is shameful for a woman to speak in church.
>
> (1 CORINTHIANS 14:34–35)

These lines come at the end of a lengthy discussion about orderly worship, with the specific focus being tongues, or ecstatic utterances, which apparently were fairly common in Corinthian worship. Paul's concern was for outsiders who visited and could not understand what was being said. To them, the service would be chaotic unless there were church members ready to interpret the

tongues that were spoken. Likewise, Paul said, any prophetic statements that were made had to be done one at a time, so that there
was time to absorb and consider what was being said. This was,
again, for the sake of the uninitiated person who wanted to learn
more about Jesus and could only do so in a service in which things
were done in some order. As Paul put it, "For God is a God not of
disorder but of peace" (1 Corinthians 14:33). A couple of verses
later, Paul picks up on this same train of thought: "Or did the
word of God originate with you?" (1 Corinthians 14:36); this leads
into more discussion about prophecy and tongues, concluding
with a summary statement: "So, my friends, be eager to prophesy,
and do not forbid speaking in tongues; but all things should be
done decently and in order" (1 Corinthians 14:39–40).

Between verses 33 and 36, though, there's a jarring interrup-
tion, as the focus turns abruptly from prophecy and tongues in
worship to women keeping quiet. To the observant reader, it
becomes even more interesting, as most modern English translations contain a footnote at the bottom of the page that says something like this: "Other ancient authorities put verses 34–35 after
verse 40." This means that the lines about restrictions on women
speaking were not even in the same place in the earliest manuscripts that still exist. It should be noted that the books of the Bible
did not suddenly drop down from the sky, but were written by
people like Paul and then reproduced by various unknown copy-
ists. While we do not have the apostle's actual original letter, we do
have several early copies, which almost always agree with one
another, except in rare instances like this, where some have these
words about women in one place, breaking up the train of thought
about tongues and prophecy, and others in another place, at the
end after the clear closing summary. Even more intriguing is the
fact that a recently uncovered early manuscript does not contain
the controversial verses in either place, but rather in the margins
of the page. Add to this the vocabulary in these verses, which is

decidedly unlike Paul's language in the rest of the book or elsewhere ("as the law also says" is a very un-Pauline thing to say, as is
"in the churches" or "subordinate"). The result is a questionable
section being attributed to Paul.

And there's more. In the same letter to the Corinthians, Paul
opens another section on worship, "I commend you because you
remember me in everything and maintain the traditions just as I
handed them on to you" (1 Corinthians 11:2). A little later in the
chapter, he appears to continue this thought: "Now in the following instructions I do not commend you, because when you come
together it is not for the better but for the worse" (1 Corinthians
11:17). What follows is a pastoral directive on why the wealthier
members of the church should wait for the working class to come
in from their duties before beginning the communal feast: "So
then, my brothers and sisters, when you come together to eat, wait
for one another" (1 Corinthians 11:33). And yet between verses 2
and 17 is another difficult section about women needing to cover
their heads in worship—difficult because it once again breaks up
the train of thought about showing concern for others above one's
own self, especially when it comes to the communal meal, and
because the vocabulary in this section is again unlike Paul's language
in the rest of the letter or elsewhere, except in the disputed verses
in chapter 14. Paul's chief concern throughout 1 Corinthians was
the unity of the people in the church, that they should show love
toward one another as fellow members of one body. The two sections on restricting women, one of which is actually found in different places in different early manuscripts, do not fit his overall
argument, his specific train of thought in each section, or even his
typical vocabulary. Perhaps Paul did not write those sections at all;
perhaps they were added very soon after his passing so as to deal
with the challenge concerning women in positions of leadership. It
should also come as little surprise that in 1 Corinthians 12:13,
where Paul cites his famous baptismal formula—"Jews or Greeks,

slaves or free"—the third pair that is found in Galatians 3:28, "male and female," is noticeably absent.

The long-standing argument when any questions are raised about this is that there was a group of particularly troublesome women in Corinth and Paul needed to deal with them. But this doesn't explain the problems in placement and vocabulary we've just considered. And it doesn't fit Paul's clear acceptance of women in leadership as noted in his greetings in Romans 16. What makes more sense is to consider that the only way for church leaders, who were very much a product of their time, to deal with the liberation of women that came from Paul's belief that there were to be no outside distinctions in the Christian community, was to make it sound as though Paul himself had placed restrictions on women.

This strategy becomes even more obvious with the later so-called disputed letters of Paul, those letters that use very different language and appear to address issues that arose after Paul's lifetime. In some, such as the Letters to the Ephesians and the Colossians, there are "household codes" that tell wives, children, and slaves how to act as subordinated dependents in the household. Indeed, these codes are almost identical to Roman household codes of the same time, and quite different from the kind of talk that Paul used in his "undisputed" letters. And when it comes to the "pastoral letters" to Timothy and Titus, most scholars agree they were written later by someone other than Paul (though possibly with some excerpts of Paul's writing woven in). In the second chapter of 1 Timothy, for example, there is a section about how women should dress and act, so as to acknowledge their subordinate status. The sentiment here sounds very much like what we saw in 1 Corinthians: "Let a woman learn in silence with full submission. I permit no woman to teach or to have authority over a man; she is to keep silent" (1 Timothy 2:11–12).

In situations where he could not easily be edited, as with the pithy letter to Philemon that addresses the slavery issue, Paul's opponents took another tack and simply dismissed the letter as a theological lightweight, not worthy of real consideration or study. It was saved, but relegated to the back end of Paul's letters in the Christian scriptures, following the ones ascribed to him that he most likely did not write. In the shadow of household codes on how slaves should obey their masters, the letter calling on Philemon to free his slave Onesimus and welcome him as a brother in Jesus becomes invisible. Paul, the fearless advocate for unity and equality in Jesus, became known instead as the arch-conservative whose restrictions on women and slaves resulted in nineteen centuries of inequity and injustice. It could be argued that his opponents had succeeded in the ultimate spin. If Paul could not be discredited as an apostle, then the next best option for those who feared what he set in motion was to rein things in under his name, to make it sound as if he demanded adherence to the social status quo. Sadly, their strategy worked. They found a way to domesticate the radical apostle.

DEALING WITH DANGER

It has always amazed me that most people who know anything about Christianity prefer Peter to Paul. For someone who was so well-known for being a bold leader, Peter actually seemed to be easily intimidated. It is, of course, a point of record that he once denied knowing Jesus not once, but three times, to save his own skin. But that was before he was empowered by the Holy Spirit at Pentecost. After that, he was a rock, the undisputed captain of the apostles. Yet, somewhere along the way, Peter found himself in another dilemma, sitting and eating and mixing with the uncircumcised followers of Jesus as representatives from the home office came into town. Again he panicked and withdrew from those who might make him appear unclean. This made Paul furious. If everyone followed Peter's lead, Paul insisted, it would mean that the church was no different than the society around it. Paul would not let that happen. He fought, and risked disapproval for publicly challenging Peter. And yet, years later, it is Peter who remains beloved; Peter who is listed as the first pope.

We must recover Paul. Even as the "pastoral letters" were painting him as the keeper of the status quo, there were other writings, like the lesser known Acts of Paul and Thecla, that retained a spark of the fire that was in Paul, that erstwhile persecutor of the church who went on to lift it up as the place where there were no societal distinctions between members, where there was no longer "Jew or Greek, slave or free, male or female," where instead all were to be one in Jesus.

For Reflection

1. What was your impression of the apostle Paul before reading this chapter? How did you come to your opinion of him? What do you think now?

2. Paul's companion Barnabas had to vouch for him to a group of very reluctant apostles. When have you had to stand up for someone who was not welcome?

3. Paul's letters, despite their unique contexts, all touch on the need for church members to look beyond their differences and find their common identity in Christ. Why is that so difficult for people in both religious and secular systems? What groups today do it well?

For Further Reading

Borg, Marcus, and John Dominic Crossan. *The First Paul: Reclaiming the Radical Visionary Behind the Church's Conservative Icon.* New York: HarperOne, 2010.

Dunn, James D. G. *The New Perspective on Paul.* Grand Rapids: Eerdmans, 2007.

Elliott, Neil. *Liberating Paul: The Justice of God and the Politics of the Apostle*. Minneapolis, MN: Augsburg Fortress, 2006.

Longenecker, Richard N. *The Road from Damascus: The Impact of Paul's Conversion on His Life, Thought, and Ministry*. Eugene, OR: Wipf and Stock, 2002.

Malina, Bruce J., and Jerome H. Neyrey. *Portraits of Paul: An Archaeology of Ancient Personality*. Louisville: Westminster John Knox, 1996.

Robertson, C. K. *Conversations with Scripture: Acts of the Apostles*. New York: Morehouse, 2010.

2

MARY MAGDALENE

The Witness

If the Savior made her worthy, who are you
indeed to reject her?

—GOSPEL OF MARY, SAYING 9:6

Given her fame down through the ages, it's easy to imagine that Mary Magdalene must have been one of the stars of the Christian scriptures. But the truth is that she only has a little time onstage in the Gospels and none at all in the letters of Paul. In fact, her name only shows up a mere baker's dozen times—and several of those mentions refer to the same tales related by different writers. Mary was more of a cameo figure than a marquee attraction. Subsequent generations, however, not content with the gaps in Mary's story, have expanded her role into everything from reformed prostitute to Jesus's wife and the mother of his children. But the Gospels themselves reveal a different story.

GRATEFUL BENEFACTOR

To move beyond tabloid headlines and into a more accurate understanding of Mary Magdalene, let's begin at the beginning,

17

with the Gospels—starting with her first appearance prior to the events of the crucifixion. Luke 8:1–3 marks Mary's only mention before the Passion account, and the passage offers an interesting description:

> The twelve were with him, as well as some women who had been cured of evil spirits and infirmities: Mary, who hails from Magdala, from whom seven demons had gone out, and Joanna, the wife of Herod's steward Chuza, and Susanna, and many others, who provided for them out of their resources.

Here we see a grateful recipient of Jesus's healing power and compassion, determined from that point on to assist him in his ministry with the financial resources she is obviously able to provide. This tradition of faithful women offering financial assistance continues in Luke's second volume, the Acts of the Apostles, with Lydia, a dealer in purple cloths and a convert, who "prevails" upon Paul and Barnabas to use her home as a base (Acts 16:14–15). In his Letter to the Romans, Paul also mentions a deacon named Phoebe, who in the past had provided help for many Christians, including himself (Romans 16:1–2). So here in Mary Magdalene's only pre-crucifixion Gospel appearance is not a woman of ill repute but a person of means who uses her resources to support the ministry of Jesus and his apostles.

It's also clear from Luke 8:2 that Mary Magdalene acts out of gratefulness. Hers is a thankful, generous heart, and the reason for her gratitude is clear—after all, Luke says, seven demons had been driven out from her. It's reasonable to assume that Jesus is the one who initiated this exorcism, and that's exactly what Mark says in his Gospel (Mark 16:9). What is less clear, though, is the exact nature of Mary's "possession." Seven is a familiar biblical number—consider the seven days of creation in Genesis 1—referring not to a specific number of days but implying, rather, completion or totality. Whatever the precise nature of her struggles, Mary didn't simply fight her own demons; she appears to have been completely overwhelmed by them—until Jesus came to her. With his coming, she exchanged her despair for a sense of wholeness and well-being, until it was time for her to be of help to him.

APOSTLE TO THE APOSTLES

With that one exception, the Gospel passages about Mary Magdalene all focus on her time at the cross and at the empty tomb. Whatever her backstory, Mary's significance would forever be interwoven with the Passion and resurrection of Jesus. There on the mount called "the skull," looking on from a distance (Mark 15:40; Matthew 27:56; John 19:25), while the apostles are nowhere to be seen, Mary and her companions stand by Jesus to the end. Following his death, it is Mary and the other women who are found at his graveside, watching to see where he has been laid (Mark 15:47; Matthew 27:61). Mary and those with her become the living icons of Christian devotion and self-sacrifice. They had been there all along, supporting his ministry and his apostles' ministry, and when the apostles flee, Mary stays. When Joseph of Arimathea, a member of the Jewish council and a follower of Jesus, comes to bury the body in his own tomb, Mary is still there.

All this leads to that glorious moment when, on the first day of the week, Mary finds her way down to the grave to finish the burial preparations and anointing that had been postponed by observance of the Sabbath. Although the Gospels differ in several details, they all agree that it was Mary—alone in some of the tales, accompanied by companions in others—who is the first witness of the resurrection. In Mark's account, she and two others are busy asking themselves, along the way to the tomb, who would roll away the stone that sealed its entrance, when suddenly they arrive, only to find that the large stone has already been moved. Inside, a "young man dressed in a white robe" (Mark 16:5)—presumably an angel—tells Mary and the other women not to be alarmed, that Jesus has been raised from the dead.

Even more remarkably, the mysterious young man tells Mary and her friends to tell Jesus's disciples, particularly Peter, that Jesus is coming to them.

Mark's account is intriguing because it ends with Mary and the others fleeing from the tomb and saying nothing to anyone, "for terror and amazement had seized them" (Mark 16:8). This ending made little sense to many in the early Church, so some ancient manuscripts add a short ending that says the women did indeed do what they'd been told, and other manuscripts add a longer ending with details of the risen Jesus appearing to his disciples after Mary speaks to them. (This longer ending says that Jesus had cast out seven demons from her.) In both additions to Mark's original Gospel, Mary and the women are shown doing what the angel commanded, rather than—as in the original ending—being frozen in fear.

In Matthew's Gospel, Mary Magdalene, accompanied by another Mary, witnesses the divine earthquake and the angel rolling the stone away, even as the guards at the tomb are paralyzed with fear. As in Mark, the angel bids the women peace, tells them that Jesus has been raised, and commands them to go and tell the news to the disciples. In this account, the women leave the tomb quickly, "with fear and great joy" (Matthew 28:8), and on their way to the disciples encounter the risen Jesus himself. Taking hold of his feet, they worship Jesus, who urges them to go and tell his disciples. Presumably they do, since Matthew ends his Gospel with Jesus commissioning the apostles on the mountaintop, reminding them that he would be with them always, "to the end of the age" (Matthew 28:20).

Luke's account of the Easter-morning events is a bit different. It records that several women, some named and some anonymous, accompany Mary. Arriving at the tomb, they're perplexed to find the stone already moved away and the body gone. Suddenly, not one but two men in dazzling clothes appear and tell them that Jesus has been raised: "Why do you look for the living among the dead?" (Luke 24:5). Though the angels don't command the women to bring the news to the disciples, Mary and her friends do so on their own, only to have the eleven apostles dismiss the news as "an idle tale" (Luke 24:11). It's only Peter who runs to the tomb to see for himself and, finding only the linen burial cloths, goes home amazed.

In the Gospel of John, Mary is alone as she goes to the tomb and finds the stone removed. She immediately runs to tell Peter and "the disciple whom Jesus loved" (John 20:2), and these two in turn go to see for themselves, then return to their homes. Mary, though, stays there, "weeping outside the tomb" (20:11), when two angels in white sitting where Jesus had lay ask her why she's crying. "They have taken away my Lord," she replies, "and I do not know where they have laid him" (20:13). Turning, Mary sees Jesus himself, though she doesn't recognize him, perhaps because his post-resurrection appearance is altered in some way. In fact, she thinks he's the gardener and asks him, "Sir, if you have carried him away, tell me where you have laid him, and I will take him away" (20:15)—a heartfelt plea from one who loves Jesus deeply. When Jesus responds simply by saying her name, Mary recognizes him immediately (20:16). Unlike the scene in Matthew's Gospel, here Jesus urges Mary not to touch him because he has not yet ascended to his Father. Mary goes and tells the disciples, "I have seen the Lord!" (John 20:18).

Each of these resurrection accounts, which complete Mary Magdalene's appearances in the New Testament, show, despite differences in details, that Mary is not only the first witness of the resurrection, but also the messenger who brings the good news of the risen Jesus to the skeptical apostles. Whether with trepidation or joy, alone or with other women, it's Mary who tells Jesus's friends what she's seen and experienced. Mary Magdalene—that loyal follower who contributed to Jesus's ministry, stood by him at his crucifixion, witnessed his body's burial—became apostle to the apostles.

PURE SPIRITUAL WOMAN

In recent years, there's been an upsurge of interest in Mary Magdalene and increased attention to ancient nonbiblical documents that mention her. These documents often elevate Mary to the position of a closer confidante to Jesus than Peter and the apostles. There are five particular documents to note.

The Dialogue of the Savior is a treatise found in the Nag Hammadi Library, part of a collection of ancient manuscripts that had eroded through the centuries, making sections impossible to read. However, in this document, Mary, along with Judas (not Iscariot) and Matthew, asks many questions of Jesus and shows great wisdom in her responses to him: "She spoke this utterance as a woman who understood everything."[1]

Pistis Sophia, translated literally as "faith wisdom," written as early as the second century, was rediscovered in the eighteenth century, separate from the Nag Hammadi collection. During a question-and-answer session in the document, Mary takes an active role, asking four out of five of the questions, overshadowing the apostles. She is described by Jesus himself as "one whose heart is set on heaven's kingdom more than all your brothers." Later in the book, Peter shows his exasperation with Mary who, he asserts, talks all the time. Mary herself later admits to Jesus, "My master, I understand in my mind that I can come forward at any time to interpret what Pistis Sophia has said, but I am afraid of Peter, because he threatens me and hates our gender." As in *The Dialogue of the Savior*, Mary receives high commendation from Jesus: "Well done, Mary, pure spiritual woman."[2]

The Gospel of Philip is part of the Nag Hammadi collection and contains two highly controversial sayings:

> There were three who always walked with the Lord: Mary his mother and her sister and Magdalene, the one who was called his companion. His sister and his mother and his companion were each a Mary.
>
> (SAYING 36)[3]

Another fragment with gaps says:

> The companion of the [gap] Mary Magdalene. [Gap] her more than [gap] the disciples [gap] kiss her [gap] on her [gap].
>
> (SAYING 59)[4]

Though seemingly provocative, the word "companion" here means "associate," not "lover," in the original Coptic, despite modern speculation, as in the novel *The Da Vinci Code*.

The Gospel of Thomas, a work that's become popular in recent years, consists of 114 sayings of Jesus, with no deeds, miracles, stories, or Passion account. Some of the sayings are the same as or similar to ones found in the four official, or canonical, Gospels, but there are also other wisdom statements that clearly arose from the Gnostic tradition, that rival faith system that emphasized spiritual realities over the material world and spoke of a secret knowledge—or—*gnosis*—that enabled the one who obtained this knowledge to move beyond this lesser realm. In this collection of sayings, Mary is found twice, first early on, in saying 21, where she asks Jesus, "Whom are your disciples like?" Then, in the final saying, a dialogue between Peter and Jesus ends with Peter saying, "Let Mary leave us, for women are not worthy of life." Jesus's response is problematic: "I myself shall lead her in order to make her male, so that she too may become a living spirit resembling you males. For every woman who will make herself male will enter the kingdom of heaven."[5] This is a defense of Mary perhaps, but hardly a cry of liberation and equality for her as a woman!

The Gospel of Mary was discovered in Egypt in the late nineteenth century, but due to several unfortunate circumstances it remained unavailable to the public until a Coptic edition was finally published in 1955, though there are also shorter, earlier Greek manuscripts of the document. The main purpose of the Gospel is to encourage anxious followers of Jesus to proclaim the good news, but it depicts Mary in a leadership role. Recognizing her close bond with Jesus, Peter asks her to teach the male disciples and she agrees: "What is hidden from you I will proclaim to you" (saying 5:7).[6] In earlier Greek fragments, Mary's gender does not seem to be a problem; Peter and the apostles simply take issue with the content of her message. But in the later Coptic version released in 1955, additional content clearly reveals a bias against women on the part of the Church's leadership. Peter, who earlier affirmed Mary, now says, "Did [Jesus] really speak privately with a woman and not openly to us? Are we to turn about and all listen to her? Did he prefer her to us?" (saying 9:4).[7] Another apostle, Levi, acknowledges that Peter has always been "hot-tempered" and challenges him and the rest to listen to her: "If the Savior made her worthy, who are you indeed to reject her?" (saying 9:6).[8]

FROM APOSTLE TO PROSTITUTE TO WIFE

Nothing in the biblical Gospels or in the later documents that mention Mary Magdalene portrays her as a prostitute. That characterization would take five centuries to be officially declared, then fourteen more centuries to be overthrown. In the Gospels, Mary is a faithful follower of Jesus and first witness of the resurrection, and in the later writings she is a leader and someone to whom Jesus had imparted special wisdom. There's a mention of possession in the Gospels, but possession doesn't equate with prostitution; in fact, one tradition holds that Mary was so chaste that the devil sent seven demons to trouble her. So how did this well-known image of Magdalene as a prostitute come to be—and why?

"Why" is the more profound question, but as for "how," the quick and simple answer is that people have conflated the passage beginning in Luke 8:1, introducing Mary Magdalene and her fellow women sponsors, with the story immediately prior to it in Luke 7:36–50. In this preceding tale, an anonymous woman who is a known "sinner" anoints Jesus's feet while he tries to explain the value of her act to Simon, his overly judgmental host. It's not terribly surprising, then, that the two stories, literally back-to-back in Luke's Gospel, would somehow become intertwined. And to make matters a bit more confusing, there's the similar passage in John 7:53–8:11 (a passage that is not even original to the Gospel, but added in later manuscripts) about the woman caught in adultery whose life is saved by Jesus when he declares to her would-be executioners, "Let the one who is without sin cast the first stone."

Mix in even more confusing factors, such as the multiple women in the Gospels with the name of Mary—besides Magdalene, there is Mary the wife of Clopas, Mary the mother of James, and, of course, Mary the mother of Jesus. In John's Gospel, for instance, the woman who anoints Jesus prior to his death is named Mary, too—not Magdalene though, but Mary of Bethany, sister of Martha and Lazarus. The profusion of Marys is not unique to the Gospels; in the first-century Palestinian region, one-quarter of Jewish women whose names are known to us were named Mary. So it becomes a little easier to appreciate how some misunderstandings could develop about which Mary is being discussed in any given passage. But none of these other Marys was known to be a prostitute either, including Mary of Bethany, who anointed Jesus. It is precisely because so much is unknown about Mary Magdalene that some have filled in the blanks in a way that suits their agendas.

This brings us to the important question of *why* some would suggest that this apostle to the apostles was actually a woman of ill repute. Women had few chances to exercise leadership or independence in first-century Mediterranean society. So there must have been a kind of liberty in following Jesus, who spoke of his community preempting the usual family and social obligations: "Whoever does not hate father or mother ... for my sake is not worthy to be called my disciple" (Luke 14:26). Far from being a negative, such a statement must have sounded freeing to women who were under the authority of father or husband or whose lives were defined by their children or brothers. And Jesus's prohibition against divorce, precisely because it was stricter than the usual understanding of the Law of Moses, was a welcome word to women, as men who followed Jesus could not dismiss their wives on a whim. At a very basic level, Jesus acknowledged women, spoke to them, befriended them. For women like Mary Magdalene, following Jesus might have offered protection, respect, and previously unthought-of opportunities.

To those men who believed women to be inferior to men, a woman with a highly visible role in the beginnings of Christianity could have been seen as a great threat. Both the Gospels and the other writings suggest that Mary did indeed hold a special place in relation both to Jesus personally and to the beginnings of Christianity. For some, this was unacceptable. She could not possibly be allowed to be seen as the equal of—or worse, superior to— the male apostles. So, it very well may have been that the historical defamation of character—the penitent but still morally stained prostitute—was intentional. It was Pope Gregory the Great who in 591 CE declared that Mary Magdalene, Mary of Bethany, and the anonymous prostitute were one and the same. And that reputation stayed with Mary Magdalene, finding its way into paintings and films, where's she's always pictured with flowing red hair, traditionally a sign of wanton ways.

In 1969, the Second Vatican Council of the Roman Catholic Church finally, though subtly, abandoned that earlier position, by changing the readings for the day from Luke 7:36–50, about the anonymous sinful woman washing Jesus's feet, to John 20:11–18, about Mary encountering the risen Jesus. But for many people, this was not enough. There was a growing interest in the idea that Mary Magdalene might have been closer to Jesus than the Church would like to admit. Indeed, some began to argue that she was even his wife. Because of the silence in the Gospels about her post-resurrection life, various tales have arisen. One tradition has it that she died in the city of Ephesus, in modern-day Turkey, and was buried in Constantinople, now known as Istanbul. A more questionable account has her traveling with Joseph of Arimathea, who buried Jesus in his own tomb, all the way to the British Isles, bringing with them the Holy Grail, the cup used at the Last Supper and then later at the foot of the cross to catch the blood of Jesus. In a variation of this tale, Mary herself is the Grail, literally carrying the seed of Jesus within her own body and eventually giving birth to his child, Sarah (and later, a son as well, some say).

Still another set of stories has Mary arriving in France, where through Jesus's and her offspring there emerged the Merovingian royal bloodline in France, continued into our own time in secret. Two different churches in France have traditionally claimed the honor of holding the real bones of Mary, although it is not necessary to cross the Atlantic to find a purported Magdalene relic, as a reliquary containing a tooth supposedly belonging to her now resides in the Metropolitan Museum of Art in New York City. The legends about Mary's more intimate relationship with Jesus are based in part on those early extra-biblical fragments, such as the passages in the Gospel of Philip about Mary being Jesus's "companion" and being kissed by him. These tidbits have become fodder for speculation and sensationalism in modern books like *Holy*

Blood, Holy Grail by Michael Baigent, Richard Lee, and Henry Lincoln, and *The Da Vinci Code* by Dan Brown.

DEALING WITH DANGER

Mary did indeed pose a threat to the early Church—and perhaps she still threatens the Church today. While in some stories she was associated with certain types of unorthodox or alternative teaching, the real challenge for many in her time was her gender itself. More than Priscilla or Phoebe or any of the women in Paul's ministry—with the possible exception of Julia/Junia in Romans 16, possibly described by Paul as an apostle in a verse disputed by scholars—Mary Magdalene was dangerous because she was nothing less than an apostolic figure. She was the first witness to the resurrection. She was there. Even Peter couldn't make that claim. She was also there at the cross when Peter himself fled and denied even knowing Jesus. She was faithful when the men in Jesus's life proved faithless. Yet Mary could not be an apostle, the Church said, for one of the chief arguments for perpetuating a male-only priesthood was that these were successors to the apostles, and Jesus only had male apostles! It is a backwards argument: she can't be an apostle because our way of operating now depends on her not having been one. Perhaps a rival faction did elevate Mary above the apostles, even above Peter, causing the more orthodox wing in the Christian movement in the early years of the Church to react and defend their own growing traditions. The hierarchy of the Roman Catholic Church has historically felt so strongly about this that they have refrained from ordaining women even to our own time, and other Christian groups have done likewise.

Most scholars think that Magdalene likely refers to Mary's hometown, Magdala, a fishing town on the edge of the Sea of Galilee, later known as a kind of resort city. But beyond being a possible reference to her home city, Magdalene also seems to have been a kind of nickname for Mary. In her only pre-crucifixion appearance in Luke's Gospel, the writer says that Mary was "called Magdalene" (Luke 8:2). The city of Magdala was also known for its tower; indeed, the name "Magdala" has at its root the Hebrew word *migdal*, meaning "tower" or "stronghold." Jerome, the fourth-century saint and scholar who translated the scriptures into Latin, said that the name also suited Mary, for there was something strong about her, like a tower. But a strong woman could be seen as a threat to a male-dominated society—and to a male-dominated Church. It could not be denied that she was the first witness of the resurrected Christ. So the only recourse for some was to cast aspersions on her character, thus elevating the former fisherman over the former whore. This tower honored by Jesus himself could not be destroyed, but enough baggage was cast on her so as to make this tower lean.

For Reflection

1. Down through the millennia, Christians have found in Mary Magdalene an astonishing variety of meanings. What does she mean to you? How does her example point you closer to the Divine?

2. Have you encountered other Mary Magdalenes—either in your own experience or in literature, current affairs, or even your own family? In what ways have they been marginalized?

3. What can our own society learn from Mary's demotion in Christian history from "apostle to the apostles" to reformed prostitute and back to heroic figure?

For Further Reading

Adam, Betty. *The Magdalene Mystique: Living the Spirituality of Mary Today.* New York: Morehouse, 2006.

De Boer, Esther A. *The Gospel of Mary: Listening to the Beloved Disciple.* New York: Continuum, 2005.

Ehrman, Bart. D. *Peter, Paul, & Mary Magdalene: The Folksayings of Jesus in History and Legend.* New York: Oxford University Press, 2008.

King, Karen L. *The Gospel of Mary of Magdala: Jesus and the First Woman Apostle.* Salem, OR: Polebridge, 2003.

Meyer, Marvin, with Esther A. de Boer. *The Gospels of Mary: The Secret Traditions of Mary Magdalene, the Companion of Jesus.* New York: HarperOne, 2006.

For a website devoted entirely to Mary, go to www.magdalene.org.

3

ORIGEN OF ALEXANDRIA

The Innovator

Now the true soldiers of Christ must always
be prepared to do battle for the truth.
—ORIGEN'S COMMENTARY ON
THE GOSPEL OF JOHN, BOOK VI, CHAPTER 3

H e was hailed by some as his generation's greatest mind and
denounced by others as its greatest heretic. Theologian, biblical scholar, teacher, author—all these are bullet points on his
impressive resume. Few could match him for productivity; he was
one of the most prolific writers of his, or any, age. And not only
Christians, but philosophers also would wrestle with the concepts
he introduced long after his death. No other Apostolic Father
would generate as much energy and anxiety as he did, without
even intellectually breaking a sweat. The great Gregory of Nyssa,
the fourth-century theologian, philosopher, and bishop of what is
now modern Turkey, called him the "prince of Christian learning,"
and the fourth-century Church historian Eusebius considered him
a hero. But he had many enemies as well, not only among heretics

of every variety, but also among Christian bishops—and even a pagan emperor! Tragic and tortuous were his final years, and in many ways he fared even worse in the period following his demise. Deposed, exiled, excommunicated, he still managed to be a key influence on many, with an entire theological system named for him, though there actually was little of his impressive and inquiring spirit in it. Whether understood or feared, admired or despised, it would be difficult to find any simple box or formula that could worthily encapsulate Origen of Alexandria.

THE PRODIGY AND THE PATRIARCH

Origen Adamantius was only seventeen when he took the reins of the Christian catechetical school in the scholarly mecca that was Alexandria, Egypt, in the third century CE. This was a remarkable achievement, especially following in the footsteps of the renowned Clement of Alexandria. But young Origen was up to the challenge, having been prepared for a life of scholarship by his father, Leonides, a scholar himself. Thanks to his father, Origen was given a first-class education, well versed in the scriptures as well as in Greek classical writings. His father gave him one other gift as well, modeling faithfulness in the face of imprisonment and, finally, a martyr's death.

Indeed, those were difficult days for followers of Jesus. The persecution that claimed the life of Origen's father was an especially bloody affair focused on Alexandria, the great city where East met West. Initiated by the Roman emperor Septimus Severus in 202, it was only one of a series of persecutions that would continue throughout Origen's life. Even as Christians endured the wrath of Severus and subsequent emperors, they also looked on with dread as barbarian tribes attacked parts of Europe, upsetting the precarious equilibrium set up by the Roman Empire. It was a time when the followers of Jesus desperately needed to stand together in a united front—yet that was the one thing they seemed unwilling to do. It was the beginning of an age of doctrinal disputes, with almost as much instability within the Christian system as there was around it. Some would say that the problem lay in the fact that Christian thought had not yet been systematized and codified, so that there was no real clarity about what was deemed acceptable doctrine and what was not. Others would counter that the problem was the start of too much stringency and not enough space allowed for the kind of speculative thinking that Origen, in particular, did so well.

In the midst of this period of change and uncertainty, Bishop Demetrius, patriarch of Alexandria, gave his official blessing to young Origen as head of the catechetical, or religious formation, school. For twelve years, Origen and his school thrived. His own commitment to exploration and inquiry attracted new Christians—catechumens—and pagans alike, and the school grew. He even made the time to continue his own study, attending lectures under renowned scholars such as Ammonius Saccas, a Neoplatonist who taught such philosophical luminaries as Plotinus. When he finally had the help he needed to run the school, Origen sought out rabbis to help him learn Hebrew, in order to become more adept in his translation of the scriptures. Although the one-time prodigy offered an "Ivy League" education to his students, it was no "ivory-tower" experience for either teacher or students. Indeed, many of those who studied with him went on to die martyrs' deaths. And even as Origen the son had once exhorted his own father to persevere in his faith to the end, now Origen the teacher stood by his students, encouraging them in the midst of their final struggles. With each death, Origen the academic further learned that Christian faith is not simply a theoretical exercise.

The persecutions only grew in intensity, and eventually, following increased attacks on Alexandria by order of Emperor Caracalla, Origen was forced to leave both school and city, settling as an expatriate in Palestine, in the city of Caesarea. There, this lay scholar impressed Alexander, bishop of Jerusalem, who appointed Origen as a preacher in that region, an unusual call for someone who was not ordained. With this appointment, Origen began to learn firsthand the dark side of Church politics. For whatever the reason—whether out of envy of Origen himself or wounded pride that another bishop was "stealing" his protégé—an irritated Demetrius of Alexandria called Origen back from Palestine to Alexandria as a measure of ecclesiastical discipline. Origen settled back into his teaching and his writing. But troubles were far from over with Demetrius.

In the years ahead, Origen made other trips—for example, to Rome and Antioch—but it was one particular journey that took him through Caesarea, today midway between Tel Aviv and Haifa, where his life would take a dramatic turn. Like Alexander of Jerusalem, Theoctitus, bishop of Caesarea, was deeply impressed with Origen. With Alexander joining him, Theoctitus took the unexpected step of ordaining Origen a priest. It proved to be the breaking point for Demetrius, who viewed this action as a slap in the face to his own authority. Origen did not see the rude homecoming that awaited him when he returned to Alexandria. Demetrius quickly made it clear that the new priest was not welcome in his territory, and it was not long before the patriarch pushed Church councils to declare Origen's ordination irregular and have him deposed as a priest. If this was not enough, Demetrius had him banished from Alexandria as well. As St. Jerome, the famed biblical translator, later made clear, Origen's excommunication from Alexandria had nothing to do with anything he taught or wrote. The conflict with Demetrius, though, was but a summer shower compared with the storm that was yet to come.

FIRST PRINCIPLES AND DEEPER MEANINGS

Looking back, it is ironic that Origen would later be considered a heretic. From the start, he was committed to providing theological tools to stand against the various heresies that existed in those early days of the Church, the most prevalent of which were known collectively as Gnosticism. As the word implies, this system focused on "knowing" (consider the word's opposite, "agnostic"), linking salvation to knowledge of divine mysteries. Christian Gnostics spoke of the divide between the Divine Source of life and spirit, known by Jesus, the enlightened one, and a lesser god or "demiurge" found in the Hebrew scriptures, the one responsible for the material world with all its limitations, sickness, and death. New scriptures were created that reflected Gnostic principles, such as the Gospel of Thomas and the Gospel of Mary. The common thread in all these was some secret wisdom passed along by Jesus to a key follower but unknown by the larger group of disciples, the ones who were the foundation of the one, holy, catholic, and apostolic Church that served as Gnosticism's rival. That secret wisdom was needed to break out of the limitations of the world of matter and flesh and discover the realm of true spirit. As a religious system, Gnosticism was attractive to many because it offered a philosophical complexity that was difficult for less sophisticated Christians to refute.

This is precisely why Origen felt so strongly about entering the fray. Early in his scholarly ministry, even before the political difficulties with Demetrius, Origen had been working on a theological counteroffensive to Gnosticism. The result, *On First Principles* (*De Principiis*), was in many ways the first attempt by anyone to create a systematic theological basis for Christianity, and Origen did so by drawing on his own learning, which included some of the same pagan philosophical wisdom that was being appropriated by his Gnostic opponents. He was particularly familiar with, and appreciative of, Plato's concepts, having become acquainted with the Greek philosopher from his days of study under Ammonius Saccas and others. Today, we only have part of this great work, as the original Greek manuscript that Origen wrote now exists only in fragments. We have to rely on a Latin translation prepared by Origen's strong supporter, Rufinus. Still, even with some questions about what was lost in the process, it is clear that *On First Principles* was an exploratory, speculative work. This is difficult for some Christians today to appreciate, especially those who value certainty over speculation. For Origen, however, it was expected that a philosophically trained believer was still free to engage in reasonable investigation.

Origen's theological exploration, of course, was a response to what he heard and read from Gnostic scholars. So he touched on several key areas of dispute, including the Trinity—the nature of God as three-in-one—the question of souls, human free will, and the ultimate restoration of all things. In each of these areas, Origen combated what he saw as the dangers in Gnostic teaching but, interestingly, left himself open for later accusations of heresy from other orthodox Christians. Regarding the divine nature, for instance, Origen affirms the triune nature of God as Father, Son (Jesus), and Holy Spirit. But he further describes these using a language of hierarchy that clearly reflects Plato's theories: "The God and Father, who holds this universe together, is superior to every being that exists … the Son, being less than the Father, is superior to rational creatures alone (for he is second to the Father), the Holy Spirit is still less, and dwells within the saints alone."[1] Origen further suggests that Jesus was one soul among many, many others, all of which emanated from the Divine Source, who is God the Father. All the others fell from grace except the Jesus-soul, which alone used free will to remain within the divine existence.

If this sounds to modern ears very much like what the Gnostics claimed, it is important to note that it sounded that way to many of Origen's contemporaries too. The chief difference between then and now is that we have eighteen more centuries' worth of formulas, creeds, and confessions—and all the theological battles that went into their respective creations—while Origen was in the process of helping create a substantive theological system when none yet existed, when the only clear formulas were being put forth by the extremists, the Gnostics. Unlike many of his contemporaries, Origen was both courageous enough to take on the Gnostics directly and innovative enough to use some of their same tools in order to reach improved conclusions. For though his hierarchy sounded like Gnostic ideas of spiritual emanations, Origen went further and spoke of the unique nature of each soul that came from God and was being wooed back to God through Jesus's redemptive work. His understanding of the unique, individual nature of a soul actually formed the beginning basis for our modern concept of human personality. What made him so effective, and seemingly so dangerous, was his ability to tap into pagan concepts and "Christianize" them.

But Origen had much more in his arsenal beyond pagan philosophy. His first love and his greatest asset was scripture itself. Here, in the arena of biblical study, Origen was without peer. Remember that at this point in Christian history, just as theological principles had not yet been organized in a clear, systematic way, so too there was not yet a hard and fast "canon," or authorized collection, of scriptural texts. The books that eventually would constitute what we call the New Testament existed, of course, alongside the books of the Hebrew scriptures, but there were many other books floating around that sought official recognition as sacred texts, too. Everything was still fairly fluid. Origen helped in the sifting process by offering his own thoughts on the various contending books.

Regarding the number of Gospels to be recognized as authoritative, Origen was clear and absolute in his answer: "The Church has four, heresy a great many." He admitted the need to read these other Gospels, such as the Gospel of Thomas, a Gnostic favorite then and now, in order to not appear "ignorant" when opponents referred to these texts. However, none were to be accepted but "what the Church has recognized." The Bible indeed shaped the Church, but Origen makes it clear that the Church also shaped the Bible. This is evident in his own development of thought about certain books written by those who came to be known as the Apostolic Fathers. While still living in Alexandria, he believed books like the Epistle of Barnabas, the *Didache* or Teaching of the Twelve Apostles, and the popular *Shepherd of Hermas* to be "divinely inspired" and thus included among the authorized texts. But after moving to Caesarea, he saw that Christians there did not recognize these books in the same way and eventually changed his opinion. The crucial step of official recognition was not a single person's stamp of approval but rather reflected the way the Church at large understood and related to the texts. It is interesting that of the books that did finally make it into the New Testament canon, Origen had questions about the Epistle of James, as well as the Second Letter of Peter and the Second and Third Letters of John. Others would agree with him. (Even as late as the sixteenth century, Martin Luther, never shy with his opinions, referred to James as "an epistle of straw.") As for the issue of authorship of books that did make it into the canon, Origen recognized the difficulty with some; of the Letter to the Hebrews, he said, "only God knows" who wrote it.

Regarding the question of *how* scripture was to be interpreted, Origen offered a threefold system that was clear—but threatening to some people. First of all, he reminded Christians that interpreters of scripture must rely not on their own thinking, but on "the rule of the Church instituted by Christ."[2] No one individual or small group could say with authority what a text meant. Instead, it was crucial to hear what the larger body of members throughout the Church thought. This was not exactly democracy, but it did provide checks and balances by the larger whole as it sought divine understanding. In this way, Origen pictured the Church reflecting Jesus the way the moon reflects the light of the sun. Outside the

Church and its members' collective wisdom, he implied, there could only be darkness—hardly heretical stuff!

His actual approach to interpreting scripture is where the controversy lay. Using terms borrowed from the Greek philosopher Plato, Origen spoke of the body, soul, and spirit of scripture, referring to the literal/grammatical, the moral, and the spiritual/allegorical sense of scripture. It was his firm conviction that scripture must be interpreted in a manner worthy of God, who is the ultimate author of the sacred text. People today often speak of the spirit of the law trumping the letter of the law. Even so, Origen argued that if a particular scriptural text expressed something that in the plain grammatical sense would be either impossible for, or undeserving of, a good and perfect God, then the only logical solution was to interpret that particular text in a nonliteral, allegorical or symbolic way. Origen advocated this approach to biblical analysis not because he doubted the divine inspiration behind the scriptural texts, but precisely because he did believe that this was the Word of God. If the scriptures were of God, they had to be true, just as God is true. In modern times, some have used this line of reasoning to conclude that the only appropriate way to read scripture is in a literal sense, even if the result is somehow quite ludicrous. There are no errors in the Bible, they say, so any logical or scientific facts that oppose what is said there must be wrong. Origen, a premodern scholar, came to the opposite conclusion: any apparent contradictions and imperfections we find in scripture actually point us to a deeper way of understanding what is written. This deeper way, Origen said, is through allegory. As he put it, no passage can be read solely in its "corporal" sense if it leads the reader to an absurd or unworthy image of God.

HERO ... OR HERETIC?

By the mid-third century, Origen had fought more than his share of battles. For some, the banishment by Demetrius had tainted his reputation. His writings had made still others nervous and inquisitive about how orthodox his beliefs were. But he also had more than his share of friends and admirers, indeed many who so respected what he said that they collected his writings on the one hand to combat Gnosticism and on the other hand to strengthen the faithful, especially those facing martyrdom. By the time he was in his sixties, Origen had already penned an amazing array of biblical commentaries, homilies and teachings, theological treatises, rational defenses for Christianity, letters of encouragement, and notes of admonition. Still writing and teaching, he found himself with one more hurdle to overcome.

In January 250, the Roman emperor Decius issued an edict for the suppression of Christianity, arguing that it was "for the safety of the empire." The edict called for Christian bishops and leaders to perform a pagan sacrifice. If they refused, the consequences would be dire. The renowned Origen was arrested, imprisoned, tortured, and sentenced to death. Facing the worst, he stood his ground heroically, living out the kind of witness he had described in letters to many others who had faced martyrdom before him. But his body could not equal his spirit's resolve. The emperor's death in battle a year later resulted in freedom for Origen, but it was not soon enough. Shortly thereafter, Origen himself died, his body having endured more than it could take.

Those who had respected him in life praised him in death. Gregory of Nazianzus and Basil of Caesarea, two of the greatest Christian leaders and theologians in the Eastern part of the Church, collected many of Origen's teachings in a book known as the *Philocalia*. Others cited him in response to the ever-present threat of heresy, which seemed to grow and multiply into a smorgasbord of "isms"—Arianism, Sabellianism, Pelagianism, Nestorianism, Apollinarianism. Proponents of these alternatives to mainline Christianity seemed to come from every direction to attack Origen's faith system. The most deadly barbs against Origen, however, came from mainline, orthodox Christians, who attacked another "ism" based on extreme versions of some of his teachings. Origenism, as it came to be called, endured these attacks in waves, the first occurring in the mid- to late fourth century, more than a hundred years after Origen's death, and the next coming two hundred years after that. The key points of debate centered on Origen's allegorical interpretation of scripture and his apparent subordination of the persons in the Trinity.

It is important to note that these were the years in which the Christian canon of scripture was still being assembled and the creeds that defined for successive generations the nature of the Trinity and the person of Jesus were being drafted. Origen's teachings— or rather an exaggerated version of them in Origenism—were part of a larger debate that involved many players. And throughout these debates, personal enmity, envy, and power struggles between the various combatants exacerbated whatever genuine differences in theology might have existed. The machinations of one monk who wanted to stir things up resulted in a falling-out between two of Origen's admirers, Rufinus and Jerome. While the former remained loyal to the memory of Origen and what he understood as his true teachings, Jerome, always fearful for his reputation, reversed his earlier position of admiration for the great theologian. Their shattered friendship was but one casualty in the bitter Church wars that raged during this time. A much greater casualty was Origen's reputation. He who had given the Church tools to examine itself and its beliefs, who exemplified an inquiring mind and discerning heart, would be condemned by many as a father of heresies, while others would simply regard him with suspicion.

THE RESTORATION OF ALL THINGS

In the end, there was one important theme that lay at the very heart of all of Origen's thinking and became the most controversial of all his teachings. It was his concept of *apokatastasis*, or the "restoration of all things." Grounding this in biblical passages like 1 Corinthians 15:25–28, "that God may be all in all," Origen argued that the love of God is so great, so powerful, that even the hardest heart will one day melt before it. As he put it, "We think that the goodness of God, through the mediation of Christ, will bring all creatures to one and the same end."[3] His opponents in life and after his death condemned this as universalism and a denial of human free will. After all, Origen suggested that the devil himself would one day achieve salvation.[4] This reeked of heresy to many critics then and now, but Origen was committed to the notion that evil is not the opposite of good, but rather the absence of good. To "choose" evil made little sense to him, for it meant acting out of ignorance of good. After one has been educated in what is good, then the only reasonable free choice is for good. For Origen, this could take a long time—for some souls, perhaps more than a single lifetime. This led to his notion of a kind of reincarnation, in which it could take a soul multiple ages to experience fully and finally the overwhelming love of God—hence the restoration of all things in the end.

DEALING WITH DANGER

Origen's curse, a later writer said, was that he was an innovator in an age when innovation was automatically suspect—not unlike our own, some may say. While others would go on to be canonized for their adherence to certainty and their zeal to fight all others, Origen would forever be viewed as somehow tainted. He approached the mysteries of God through exploration and speculation, always immersing himself in scripture while also making use of secular wisdom. Whether one declares him to be a hero or a heretic, it is important and somewhat ironic to note that his condemnation came in large part because of his belief in the overpowering love of God. Even as others were condemning and excommunicating him as well as one another, Origen continued to maintain that the face of God in Jesus is the face of love. It is little wonder that a later admirer would say that he would rather be in hell with Origen than in heaven with some of those other saints who were so certain of themselves and so quick to condemn others. Of course, if Origen heard this, he would gently remind his admirer that thanks to the love of God, there ultimately will be no need for hell anyway.

For Reflection

1. The struggles Origen faced were partly the result, not of theological disputes, but of rivalries and personality clashes. How do such things still cause problems, and what can you do to encourage honest communication when faced with these personal resentments?

2. Origen's most controversial belief was that even the devil would one day be won over to God's overwhelming love. What do you think about that?

3. Another hot-button issue introduced by Origen was his own version of reincarnation, in which human beings are reborn until the time when they finally accept the transforming love of God. Why is this idea even now appealing to some and repulsive to others?

For Further Reading

Crouzel, Henri. *Origen: The Life and Thought of the First Great Theologian.* Translated by A. S. Worrell. New York: T. & T. Clark, 1989.

Ehrman, Bart D. *Lost Christianities: The Battles for Scripture and the Faiths We Never Knew.* New York: Oxford University Press, 2005.

Kannengiesser, C. *Origen of Alexandria: His World and His Legacy*. Edited by William L. Peterson. Notre Dame: University of Notre Dame Press, 1988.

Also see Origen's own writings in *The Ante-Nicene Fathers*, Alexander Roberts and James Donaldson, eds. Grand Rapids: Eerdmans, 1994.

✠

4

FRANCIS OF ASSISI

The Radical

All the darkness in the world cannot extinguish the light from a single candle.
—THE LITTLE FLOWERS OF ST. FRANCIS

He is, with little doubt, the most beloved of Christian saints: a friend to the animals, a preacher to the birds, the great ecological hero. Yet in his own lifetime, Francis of Assisi was so threatening to the political and religious powers that he was "fired," removed as head of the order he himself had founded, and encouraged to simply be a living saint and leave the real work to more worldly colleagues. Francis's name would become a household word, but what he did—and what he tried to do—would be quietly swept under the rug by those who canonized him.

KNIGHT IN SHINING ARMOR

He was born Giovanni Bernardone, son of a prosperous but not very popular Italian merchant and his possibly French-born wife. His address was the city of Assisi and his backyard the rolling

Umbrian hills, ethereal in their gray-green beauty. Pietro Bernardone was hardly the two-dimensional caricature of greed that later legend would paint him, but there does seem to have been some kind of disconnect between father and son from early on. Giovanni—or rather Francesco or Francis, as his father, who loved French ways, would call him—wanted more than the life of a merchant. He sought instead the chivalrous life of a knight, but he was no military genius. In fact, he really had the soul of a poet. But he sought the glory that comes with a knightly vocation and had a personal charisma that attracted other young seekers to his side.

Francis not only had drive; he also had opportunity. Living in the early thirteenth century, in the age of the Crusades, there were plenty of chances for a young man attracted to the life of adventure and gallantry. When Pope Urban II called for the First Crusade against the Muslim occupiers of the Holy Land in 1095, the knights are said to have responded by crying, "God wills it!" Warriors in great numbers went forth into battle, some bored with their former life, some seeking the treasure they'd heard about, still others convinced that they had a holy cause, certain that God was on their side. Many of those who went were soon disillusioned by what they found and disturbed by what they themselves did. In one case, warriors from the Western part of the Christian world found themselves slaughtering not only Muslim "infidels" but also fellow Christians from the East whose thinking and beliefs were different from theirs.

One did not have to go all the way to Jerusalem, however, to seek glory—or to find disillusionment. Young Francis enlisted in a more local war between Assisi and neighboring Perugia. After a fall from a horse, Francis the would-be knight became Francis the prisoner of war. Languishing in prison, his dreams of glory faded, and when he eventually made his way back to Assisi, all who encountered him saw that he was a changed man. Indeed, they spoke of a strange malady that seemed to possess him. He appeared to be only a shell of a man.

Although he was born in 1181, it was around the year 1205 or 1206 that the Francis whom the world would come to know came into existence. After the horrors of war and imprisonment, after the isolating illness of his mind and soul, a series of events transpired that gave him new purpose. It is a story of conversion in multiple steps, each one almost cinematic in its feel. There is the mystical occurrence in front of the crucifix in the church at San Damiano, where he heard Jesus charge him, "Repair my church." There is the raucous scene in the center of Assisi, when he gave to the poor with reckless abandon all manner of goods and treasures from his father's storehouse. There is the dramatic moment in the public square where, surrounded by a crowd of nosy onlookers, he found himself on trial before Bishop Guido. There, he shed his clothes, his possessions, his very name, and it was a naked, reborn Francis who left home that day to start a new life.

That new life, however, would not be spent alone. Even as he began literally repairing churches, Francis was soon joined by others who shed their titles and possessions and joined him. First, it was Bernard and Peter Catanii. Then came Giles, then Philip and two others. It wasn't long before enough men joined that Francis found himself writing a simple Rule of Life to help focus their life together and push them even more to live out the gospel message that had changed him. It was not a monastery that Francis founded; it was a transformed way of life.

LADY POVERTY

Francis's group, or order, was something altogether new among religious orders. For one thing, he and his followers didn't stay in one place as Benedictine or Augustinian monks did, praying in a sequestered setting. No, Francis wanted his followers to be out among the people, moving among them as itinerant preachers and servants of all. Even the name he gave to the group said much about his view of their role and mission: the Order of Friars Minor or, literally, the "Little Brothers." He did not term himself or anyone else as a "Father Abbot," for all were to see themselves as brothers, serving one another and the world around them. Like monks belonging to other more familiar Orders such as the Augustinians or Benedictines, Francis's followers embraced the vows of obedience and chastity. But it was Francis's more zealous approach to the third monastic vow—poverty—that would truly define the Friars Minor.

Lady Poverty, as Francis would refer to this way of life, was the most exquisite, most precious lady to whom he and his brothers could pledge themselves. This was not simply some austere asceticism, for no high-living hedonist ever displayed such joy in the face of great wealth as Francis continually showed in his embrace of poverty. There was actually great practicality in his passion. When asked by the bishop of Assisi about the difficulty of a life devoid of any possessions, Francis responded, "If we possessed property, Your Grace, we would need arms to defend it."[1] Francis had discovered the truth that eluded, and still eludes, the vast majority of people: we do not possess things; they possess us. As long as we have something, we are always in danger of losing it. Francis owned nothing and, as a result, was a liberated person, free to love God, free to reach out to his fellow human beings and, indeed, even to the birds and animals with whom he would be forever associated.

Lady Poverty may have caused a breach between Francis and his more material-minded father, but she opened his eyes to a much larger family where "Brother Sun, Sister Moon," and all of creation were his siblings. It is in this context that Francis loved not only all the men and women he met, but also the birds to whom he preached, the wolf he calmed, the animals who found a friend and protector in him. All who came into the presence of this

Poverello, this "little poor man," sensed the ineffable joy that seemed to radiate from him.

REBEL WITH A CAUSE

Such joy was contagious, and people began to join Francis and his Little Brothers in their simple life. This made some religious and civic leaders a bit nervous. After all, it had not been long since a sectarian group known as the Cathari or Cathars had been flourishing in parts of France, the Rhineland, and northern Italy, right before Francis came of age. That group's name literally meant "pure ones," although the group referred to itself simply as "Good Men and Women." They were dualists, believing in a strong divide between all things spiritual and material, and the time of their emergence as a populist movement paralleled one of the Western Church's most decadent periods. Their focus on poverty and simplicity was a direct challenge to the Church hierarchy's fixation on wealth and power. To the pope and other Church leaders, the Cathars were dangerous heretics, as people were joining them in droves and leaving behind the Church as well as their civic obligations. Eventually, an entire Crusade and a full round of Inquisitions would decimate the movement, but in Francis's time, the Cathars were by no means fully out of the picture, and anyone looking or sounding like them was suspect.

Francis was undoubtedly aware of this as he began his mission, and it is to his great credit that he bridged the worlds of Lady Poverty and the very wealthy Church to which he remained all his life a loyal member. But that doesn't mean he didn't make institutional leaders very nervous. For one thing, though he claimed loyalty to the Church and respect for civil authorities, his own behavior appeared extreme and bore more than a passing resemblance to the dangerous heresy of the Cathars. The story of the naked Francis bidding adieu to his old, normal life was an evocative image. But what was most disconcerting to authorities was the great number of those who caught his contagion—not just the people on the fringe of society, but many impressionable young men of the cities, leaving their former lives with no consideration of the consequences. Families, city officials, Church leaders all watched with incredulity as their best and brightest latched on to this crazy man's vision and exchanged a life of promise for a very unconventional existence. Those who might otherwise have become lawyers, knights, or wealthy merchants instead were preaching on the streets and begging for scraps to eat … and doing so with great joy. This may not have subscribed to the Cathar heresy, but they certainly looked suspicious.

FRANCIS AND CLARE: IT'S COMPLICATED

Lady Poverty was Francis's great love, but there was another woman with whom he shared his heart, and their relationship challenged conventional mores and only increased the anxiety of authorities. Thirteen years Francis's junior, Clare was born to Count Scifi, wealthy descendent of an ancient Roman family who owned a large palazzo in Assisi, as well as a castle on the slope of nearby Mount Subasio. Clare was only eleven when she first encountered the young man who was seemingly mad. It would be years before she would see where his supposed madness had led him, before she realized that she had been searching all her life for what he had found. Her desire to understand led to clandestine, chaperoned night meetings between Francis and Clare.

A full year's worth of these nocturnal discussions passed before Clare finally followed her heart's desire. Like a secret bride preparing to elope, on a prearranged night she sneaked out of her home through the "door of death," the little side door that was opened only to carry out the dead. It was an appropriate exit, for she was about to embark on a new life. Dressed in satin, she appeared before Francis and the Little Brothers, exchanging her fine dress for a course woolen habit and cutting her beautiful hair.

The vows that Francis had once made before God, Clare now made as well. It was indeed her wedding night, not to Francis but to the same Jesus who had first claimed him.

It wasn't long before Clare's younger sister Agnes ran off and joined her, and others followed. The townspeople were mystified and a bit unnerved. Now it wasn't only up-and-coming young men who were joining Francis, but otherwise sane young women as well. But even more disconcerting was what Clare's conversion meant for the role of women. After all, if she had had her way, Clare would have jumped into the apostolic life that the Friars Minor lived. But she was forbidden by culture and custom from the way of preaching and begging that the brothers were living. As a woman, she and her sisters had to be cloistered. Francis led her first to a Benedictine convent, but it was quickly evident that this was not the place for her. Instead, she and Agnes settled in the chapel of San Damiano, the place where Francis once heard Jesus call him to repair his Church. There the "Poor Clares" found their spiritual home.

Now, there was nothing new about the cloistered life, and in earlier years there had been influential nuns. Clare was different, though—not so much because she broke out of this model, but because she was more than willing to do so. Remember that if Clare had been able to fulfill her heart's desire, she would have followed the way of Lady Poverty in the same way as the Friars Minor. More than this, Clare would have spent much more time with Francis than was deemed appropriate. Indeed, their relationship raised the eyebrows of those who couldn't understand the intense spiritual intimacy that existed between the two. Some have said that, despite the many other followers who joined Francis, Clare was the only one who truly understood him, because she alone truly shared his joyful, thankful heart.

It is interesting that Franco Zeffirelli, in his 1972 film *Brother Sun and Sister Moon*, chose as Clare the same actress he had used in an earlier movie, *Romeo and Juliet*. Whatever his directorial reasons in choosing the same actress to play both Juliet and Clare, the two situations are indeed analogous. As with Shakespeare's star-crossed lovers, Francis and Clare found that those around them did not understand or appreciate their spiritual friendship. Francis made many visits to Clare's community at San Damiano, until he was urged by the Church's hierarchy to distance himself a bit more—after all, it just didn't look good. Then as now, intimacy between men and women was viewed by most Christians only in sexual terms. But the relationship between Francis and Clare was far deeper and more intimate than that of lovers. It was a relationship only possible for two individuals whose hearts were already so completely immersed in Jesus's love, which means it was a relationship that was difficult for others to define and approve. This made many in leadership very nervous.

THROUGH ENEMY LINES

There were other reasons for Church leaders to be nervous about Francis. One of the less frequently discussed, yet most notable challenges he posed to medieval Church and society involved his decision to cross enemy lines and make his way to the Holy Land to visit the Islamic sultan himself. Peacemaking was for Francis a crucial part of the gospel message. Indeed, his one great regret in life was the permanent rift between his father and himself. When faced with strife around him, he was quick to work with the dissenting parties to find a way toward reconciliation. Even in his poetic masterpiece, "The Canticle of Brother Sun," Francis made clear his concern for peacemaking and reconciliation. Having already completed several verses of praise to God through nature, depicting God as Brother Sun and Sister Moon, Francis heard about the enmity that had developed between the bishop of Assisi and the city magistrate. With this on his heart, Francis composed a new verse for the canticle:

> All praise be yours, my Lord, through those who grant pardon for love of you; through those who endure infirmity and tribulation. Blessed are those who endure in peace, for by you, Most High, they will be crowned.[2]

It was one thing, however, to bring about peace among fellow Christians. It was quite another matter to pass through an army of "Muhammadan infidels" in order to pursue a conversation with their leader, Sultan Malek-al-Kamil in Damietta, a city north of the river Nile. Such a decision appeared either crazy or suicidal. The fact is that Francis himself imagined when he started off that his journey might end in his martyrdom. Not only was he at peace with this possibility, he seemed to relish it, as Christian martyrs had in centuries past. But this was more than some simplistic death wish.

Rather, Francis's proposal to undergo a trial by fire before the sultan seemed to illustrate his awareness of the story of an earlier delegation of Christians who had encountered the Prophet Muhammad at Medina centuries before. There, following significant discussion about the person and Passion of Jesus, Muhammad invited the Christian visitors to join him and his companions in a ritual in which all would go through fire to show the truth of their faith claims, calling down the wrath of God on those who were wrong. Whether out of fear or reason, the Christians refused Muhammad's challenge and instead negotiated for mutual toleration. Some would say that that delegation had shown prudence, but others might argue that because of their fear an opportunity was lost.

Centuries later, standing before the sultan, Francis made it clear that he was more than willing to make up for that earlier failure. He would gladly face whatever challenge was put before him to show the strength of his hope in Christ. And should he die, he asked the sultan to attribute this only to some weakness on his part, and not a deficiency of the Christian faith. This time it was the followers of Islam who said they would not put Allah to the test, but Francis's willingness to brave death for what he believed made an impression on the sultan. This "ambassador of the Lord Jesus" did not convert the Muslim ruler, but did win his admiration, which made it possible for Francis and his followers to come and go in safety. In the process, this incident raised concerns on the part of leaders back home.

After all, for those leaders back home who were trying to generate support for the Crusades, it would hardly have been helpful for Francis to come back from the heart of enemy territory and speak of the kindness extended to him by the sultan. Indeed, to hear Francis speak of those "infidels" as friends only brought increased frustration to those who sought war. They were continuing a fight ostensibly to obtain control of the Holy Land sites. Francis's highly successful visit with the sultan, and the concessions the sultan gave to him for virtually unlimited access to those same precious sites, would undermine the motivation for extending an unwinnable war. The danger to the establishment was not that Francis offered some pie-in-the-sky vision of world peace. The true threat was that, whether through political savvy or innocent good fortune, Francis was able to produce a realistic, successful option for ending the wars. It was only a decade later, on February 11, 1229, that the sultan signed the Treaty of Jaffa with the Christian emperor, Frederick II, a direct result of the work of the little poor man of Assisi.

DEALING WITH DANGER

While it faithfully depicts the opposition that Francis faced in the early years of his ministry, Zeffirelli's *Brother Sun, Sister Moon* ends on a happy note. Pope Innocent III, most powerful of all medieval pontiffs, gives his blessing to the new order, and as the movie's closing credits begin, Francis is found out in the fields, singing his canticle once more. What the filmmaker has done fits a centuries-long pattern of remembering Francis as a beloved saint while ignoring the impact of what he did, and the opposition he faced, after those initial heady days of his ministry. In one sense, as time went on, there was much to celebrate. People joined the movement in large numbers, both the Order of Friars Minor and the Poor Clares, and many more living out a Rule of Life in their own context—men and women, lay and ordained—in what Francis called the "Brotherhood of Repentance." Although he had never set out to create new religious orders, this is effectively what happened as thousands flocked to follow the poor man of Assisi.

From Francis's standpoint, this unforeseen growth brought with it many problems. For one thing, he simply couldn't handle the numbers. As a charismatic leader of a dozen or two, he had no equal, but Francis was not prepared to organize a large operation. From the standpoint of the Church's hierarchy, this presented an excellent opportunity to form this movement into something tamer, more under the hierarchy's control. But two things had to happen. First, Francis needed to be replaced as leader of the movement. Second, a new Rule had to be provided to make the movement more manageable. This latter was needed because the existing Rule, if it could be called that, was austere and simplistic, literally a collection of scriptural texts pointing to Francis's keen desire for the Little Brothers to be itinerant preachers completely free of the encumbrances of property (as in a monastery) and prescribed ritual (as in reciting the Daily Office, prayer sessions set at specific hours throughout the day and night). Now, Francis was pushed by the Church's leadership to go off and work on a new Rule, while leaving the leadership of his order to someone else.

In his absence, Brother Elias, a devout but pragmatic person, oversaw things, and concessions began to be made. Property was accepted on behalf of the order, theological education began to be emphasized, compromises were reached to accommodate those joining the order who were unable to do all that Francis and his earliest followers had done. The result was, arguably, the only way for the order to survive into the future, but from Francis's view, when he returned from his time away, it was a betrayal of all that he believed and stood for. Seeing a stone structure being put up for the brothers to live in, Francis jumped on the roof and began hurling down stones, one by one. The parallel to Jesus's outburst in the Temple courtyard, overthrowing the tables of the money changers (Mark 11:15–19), was impossible to miss. Neither was Francis pleased with the compromises to the Rule. He made one final impassioned plea to the brothers but knew that it would not be enough.

As for his peacemaking work with the sultan, it soon became evident that this was simply going to disappear from people's memory, as if it had never happened. "Cover-up" is one way to describe the hierarchy's way of ignoring that part of Francis's ministry. Attention would instead be given to the miraculous gift of the stigmata, the physical marks of Jesus's crucifixion that appeared on the saint's body toward the latter years of his life, wounds that he tried to hide but that the Church lifted up in honor. The miracle simply set Francis further apart from ordinary Christians.

This move from human leader to "living saint" led to great frustrations for Francis. On the one hand, he was deeply revered. On the other hand, his chosen apostolic way of life was no longer emulated in the same way by those who came into the order. He was beloved and admired but, it increasingly appeared, not understood. The beggar from Assisi was becoming known as a second Jesus, yet felt increasingly abandoned and isolated from his own flock. His health deteriorated, his eyesight grew dim, and the cauterizations to the eyes prescribed by his doctor (a fairly common practice in the thirteenth century) simply added to his sufferings. In the nighttime, he could feel but not see scurrying mice trying to gnaw him, an unnerving sensation. Yet during this period of personal desolation, his legend continued to grow, as miracles came to be associated with him and stories abounded about his deep connection with animals and birds. The legend was almost complete.

As "Sister Death" approached, Francis welcomed her, even adding a final verse about death to his great canticle, which he asked to be sung as he breathed his last. A mere three years after his death, the pope canonized him, and St. Francis of Assisi, the patron of animals and ecology, soon became a household name. But to those who would listen, God's troubadour still sings, not just about the brotherhood of nature, but also about a brotherhood (and sisterhood) of people who can break through every social, economic, political, and interreligious barrier.

For Reflection

1. Before reading this chapter, what was your image of Francis? How, if at all, has that view changed now?

2. In what ways do we see our society taking seriously the notion of all of creation as "brother" and "sister"? How are we still falling short of Francis's ideals?

3. It has been said that no system can stay at the same level of intensity forever and has to be "domesticated" in order to survive. Do you agree with this? What was lost in the transition of leadership from Francis to Elias? What was gained?

For Further Reading

Armstrong, Regis J., trans. *Francis and Clare: The Complete Works.* Mahwah, NJ: Paulist Press, 1986.

Gasnick, Roy. *The Francis Book: 800 Years with the Saint from Assisi.* Indianapolis: Collier, 1980.

House, Adrian. *Francis of Assisi: A Revolutionary Life.* Mahwah, NJ: Paulist Press, 2003.

Moses, Paul. *The Saint and the Sultan: The Crusades, Islam, and Francis of Assisi's Mission of Peace*. New York: Doubleday, 2009.

Pitchford, Susan. *Following Francis: The Franciscan Way for Everyone*. New York: Morehouse, 2006.

Sabatier, Paul. *The Road to Assisi: The Essential Biography of St. Francis*. Orleans, MA: Paraclete Press, 2004.

Talbot, John Michael, and Steve Rabey. *The Lessons of St. Francis: How to Bring Simplicity and Spirituality into Your Daily Life*. New York: Plume, 1998.

5

HILDEGARD OF BINGEN

The Visionary

> I am, of course, the lyre and harp of God's
> kindness.
>
> —HILDEGARD OF BINGEN, *SOUL WEAVINGS*

Who could have predicted that in the twenty-first century, people would be downloading the music of a twelfth-century nun onto their iPods? Although Hildegard of Bingen never won a Grammy and isn't exactly a household name, she left a lasting mark—and not simply in music. In so many ways, she was something of a paradox. A visionary in more than one sense, she both received divine visions, which she described in her writings, and displayed a gift for what we today might call visioning or strategic thinking. Hailed as a pioneer for women in leadership, she also spoke repeatedly of women's weaknesses in terms that would be unacceptable today. She was a counselor to emperors and popes, an inspiration to the famous and the common, and a threat to those with small minds and petty jealousies. Revered in her own lifetime as a living saint, she failed—to this day—to make it through the official process of canonization. In so many ways, Hildegard was simultaneously a product of her age and ahead of her time, an uneducated woman in a patriarchal world and a recipient of the divine mysteries who heard the "sacred sound through which all creation resounds."[1]

AN INSECURE SERVANT

Hildegard was a prolific letter writer, and among her correspondents were many luminaries of her day. In her first letter in 1146 to the renowned author and head of the Cistercian Order, Bernard of Clairvaux, Hildegard spoke of him in an unusual way, as someone who was "secure." Pleading for his support, she described herself in self-deprecating terms as "your unworthy servant," but added a more illuminating comment, "for since I was a child I have never felt secure."[2] This is particularly interesting, for even though Hildegard lived in tumultuous times, she was largely sheltered from the political and social events swirling around her for the first forty-two years of her life.

The First Crusade against the followers of Islam in Jerusalem had passed, and Bernard himself would be the key proponent of the ill-fated Second Crusade. And there were wars of a different kind between the popes and the emperor, as the emperor's rival anti-popes challenged the Roman pontiffs in the years after the Great Schism in Christendom between Eastern Orthodoxy and Western Catholicism in 1054. Add to the mix the ugly affair of the murder of Thomas Beckett, archbishop of Canterbury, in his own cathedral at the hands of four knights acting on behalf of Beckett's former friend and patron, King Henry II. In the midst of all these tensions, a renaissance in art and learning was beginning to blossom in Europe, and thanks largely to Bernard, monastic reform was taking place. These were indeed interesting and turbulent times in which Hildegard grew up, and which she would help shape in her own important way.

She was born in Germany in 1098, the tenth child of a noble family. Feeling blessed by God, her parents chose to give Hildegard to God as a "tithe," turning her over when she was eight years old to an abbess, Jutta, in preparation for life in a convent. How different this was from the situation with Clare of Assisi, who one century later would secretly sneak off, against her family's desires, to join Francis and his followers in the monastic life. Most scholars contend that Hildegard's dedication by her parents was done with her consent, but she herself would later object strenuously to any attempt to similarly dedicate others without their express consent. In a divine directive, she notes that any offering by a parent of a child before "the age of reason" must be considered provisional, until the child is old enough to confirm or refuse. If the child then does not consent, the parent will be considered guiltless before God, having presented the child in good faith but also honoring what we may now call that child's own self-determination. Clearly, Hildegard's own situation made a lasting impression on her.

Young Hildegard proved to be a sickly child, likely as a result of the visions that had plagued her since the age of three, and she received care and help from Jutta that might not have been available had she remained at home. For her part, Jutta, daughter of a wealthy and influential count, unreservedly welcomed Hildegard and cared for her. After Jutta's death years later, Count Meginhard, brother of the late abbess, showed a similarly supportive spirit, financing Hildegard's convent in Rupertsberg, Germany. From Jutta, young Hildegard learned much, though not in the systematic way that men in her era were educated through the study of grammar, logic, and rhetoric. Hildegard's education, rather, was grounded in the liturgical rhythm of monastic life. She would later describe herself as *indocta*, usually translated as "uneducated," but her self-deprecating comments in various places in her writings belie her extensive engagement with the sacred scriptures, with Latin, even with the vernacular literature of the aristocracy. A younger contemporary, Elisabeth of Schönau, also shared visions she received in trances, but her writing lacks the learning that is evident in Hildegard's.

In the crucial years of Hildegard's formation, Jutta proved to be a worthy caretaker and mentor, and she grew in faith and wisdom as a result. In Theoderich of Echternach's *Life of Hildegard*, Jutta is described by Hildegard as someone who was totally committed to prayer, fasting, and good works. Having taken her own monastic vows around the age of fifteen, Hildegard followed Jutta to a retreat site that would become her home as well, and with Jutta's passing, the other nuns elected Hildegard to be their leader, abbess of the convent. She, in turn, made a fateful decision to share her visions with a monk-mentor, Volmar, someone she considered to be both reliable and influential. With his guidance, she finally went public with what she had seen, and the adventure that was to be her life began in earnest.

THE "GREEN" VISIONARY

It was Hildegard's remarkable visions that ultimately brought her to the attention of Church leaders such as Bernard and Pope Eugenius III. Her first collection of visions became a book titled *Scivias*, or *Know the Ways*, completed in 1151. It would eventually be joined by two more compilations, *The Book of Life's Merits* (1163) and *The Book of Divine Works* (1173). Hildegard's writings conveyed wisdom through vibrant and sometimes provocative imagery, gaining her notoriety and, with the pope's backing at the Synod of Trier in 1148, official approval by the Church. Certain thematic elements weave their way throughout her visions: images of light and animals and, most interestingly, "greenness." While the earth is often depicted as dry and lifeless in her visions, Hildegard's image of paradise is shown to be lush and moist and green. The holy life is also considered to be green, a life of hope and intentional living for God. That intentionality about the choices we make and the decisions we reach was crucial to Hildegard. It's why she was so disturbed by the thought of people being forced to join a religious order without their intentional choice. It was one thing to choose the religious life, but quite another to have it chosen for you against your wishes. This is also why she fought so vehemently—though in the end unsuccessfully—against certain decisions made by Church leaders without consulting her, such as when one of her dearest "daughters" in the order, a young noblewoman named Richardis, was transferred to another convent. Once again a decision that personally affected Hildegard was being made by others, and she was powerless to do anything about it.

But this did not stop her from having her visions and sharing them. If anything, Hildegard grew more confident and more powerful, in large part because she grew more politically savvy. She learned that it wasn't enough to state what seemed to be obvious; it was necessary to shape and dress up the message.

Hildegard likely would have appreciated twentieth-century communication expert Marshall McLuhan's assertion that "the medium is the message."[3] In her books of visions, in her songs, in her personal letters, Hildegard displayed a way with words that would be the envy of influential leaders of her time. She addressed Pope Eugenius as "gentle father," "resplendent father," and "father of pilgrims" before asking for his personal support—and flattery wasn't her only tool. By sharing the visions themselves, she made it clear that it was God, the Living Light, who was directing Eugenius to push the rest of the Church hierarchy to approve Hildegard's writing, "to make it green."[4] Eugenius was urged by that Light not to "reject the secrets" but, rather, by supporting them, to be assured that he would "live in eternity."[5] In this way, Hildegard used her visions to argue for their own approval. To reject them was to reject God's own message.

Hildegard's writings included far more than the collections of visions that made her famous. If the twelfth century is known as a time of renaissance, then Hildegard was a renaissance woman. Her prose covered everything from astronomy to medicine (*Causes and*

Cures, Physica), demonstrating an intuitive wisdom in her grasp of the realities of the physical world. Her *Play of the Virtues* is regarded as the first morality play of the medieval world, and some of her letters used allegorical imagery in a way unparalleled by other writers of the time. Her creative use of known languages was not enough, however, as is evident in her most intriguing creation, the so-called *Unknown Language.* Even a cursory glance at its glossary gives a picture of an internal logic and consistency that would have impressed *Lord of the Rings* creator J. R. R. Tolkien, architect of the "elven tongue." The mystery of how she used this private language notwithstanding, it reveals the considerable extent of Hildegard's imagination and intellect.

SYBIL OF THE RHINE

As remarkable as Hildegard's literary output was, it's what she did with her writings that made such an impact on the world around her. Fearless in her ways, she confronted popes and prelates with her visions and letters, sometimes acting as a conduit for God to speak directly to them and sometimes speaking up for herself—all while never losing a sense of devotion and obedience to the Church that was her life. Her combination of humility and confidence was a powerful one, and she seemed to know how to draw on both to make her mind known without alienating the recipients of her letters. It would be inaccurate to speak of her as a twenty-first-century woman, for the kinds of liberation and equality that are assumed now would have been unknown to Hildegard. But she spoke and acted in a way that was unusual for most women of her time and displayed an impressive degree of what we might now call self-awareness and non-anxious presence. Her nickname, "Sybil of the Rhine," was bestowed by those who increasingly sought her counsel, in politics as much as in spirituality.

To those observing the ongoing power struggles between the leaders of both the Church and the German Empire, it was increasingly obvious that wise counsel was needed. Successive popes, Eugenius III and Hadrian IV, came to Hildegard, seeking clarity in their decision making, as did local German bishops and archbishops. She corresponded not only with Church leaders, but also with Emperor Frederick Barbarossa. She continued to use self-deprecation, as was her custom from the start, but her messages grew increasingly bold as leaders made it clear that they were ready to listen. She still addressed her influential correspondents in flattering terms but now balanced the niceties with harsh warnings. To Eugenius, who had signed a treaty with the emperor that Hildegard believed to be unwise, she offered both praise as "the presider at Christ's nuptials with the Church"[6] (a fascinating image in itself) and caution that his attentions "were divided" and that he was potentially at the mercy of "feasting prelates."[7] Indeed, she said that the pope was actually in danger of losing the valuable "pearl," the people of God, to "the bear,"[8] most likely a metaphor for the emperor himself. Later, she wrote to Eugenius's successor, Hadrian, assuring him that he possessed a "ready understanding" and the "power of the strong key,"[9] but warned him of bloody battles caused by his apparent change in policy toward the emperor. She showed no reluctance to share harsh news alongside glad tidings. Even in one of her earliest visions, recorded in *Scivias*, Hildegard was unafraid to assert that people's motivations, no matter how much they tried to hide them or cover them in their own importance, "cannot be concealed from the depth and profundity of God's acute awareness."[10]

This was the secret of Hildegard's courage: no matter how powerful the one to whom she wrote, she knew that someone more powerful than she spoke through her. This imbued her writing with boldness and gave her the audacity to step out of her convent and undertake three different preaching tours, a highly unusual enterprise for a medieval Benedictine nun. Here was yet another instance where Hildegard stretched the expectations of what it meant to be a woman in the Middle Ages and provided a model for women of later eras to take up preaching and pastoral ministry. Her goal in her teaching and preaching was, as she said to the bishop of Liege, "to wash the mud from the beautiful pearls."[11]

In no other instance did she show herself to be bolder or more resolute than when it came to the local politics in which she soon found herself entangled. At issue was her own beloved convent. Not long after she had finished *Scivias*, Hildegard and her nuns left the monastery at Disibodenberg and created a space of their own in Rupertsberg. The move, however, resulted in serious problems. There were financial difficulties exacerbated by the abbot of Disibodenberg, who—opposed to their move—withheld the needed funding. This in turn made it even more difficult for the pioneering abbess and her nuns to make their new space into a true spiritual home. Some nuns simply left, discouraged by the hardships they had to endure. One of these was Hildegard's spiritual "daughter," Richardis. Hildegard wasted no time in fighting the family and political connections that took Richardis from her. Likewise, she fought for her convent's secure future by making a surprise visit to Disibodenberg's abbot and obtaining a verbal promise of financial support. When the abbot died soon thereafter, her battles started all over again with the new abbot, but Hildegard persevered. In all this, she proved herself to be a formidable foe to those who resisted her move toward greater independence. And though she lost the battle to bring back Richardis, she did at last obtain financial security for her convent.

Or so she thought.

CANONIZATION WOES

People had venerated her, and popes and emperors had sought her advice, and yet toward the end of her impressive ministry, Hildegard found herself actually cast outside the church itself. It all started innocently enough. The nuns had allowed a deceased young nobleman to be buried in their convent cemetery. He had been excommunicated, but at the end of his life was reconciled to the Church and even received the sacraments from a priest. Somehow, news of his readmittance to the Church's favor did not reach certain leaders—or they chose to ignore the claim of reconciliation. Diocesan leaders from Mainz argued that this nobleman had died as an excommunicant and should not receive Christian burial. When they ordered the body to be removed from the convent cemetery, Hildegard balked. Perhaps it seemed to her to be one more instance of powerful people making decisions for someone who could not answer for himself. Or perhaps she did not appreciate one more intrusion by male leaders into her convent's affairs. Whatever her reasons, Hildegard of Bingen was determined to stand against these prelates of Mainz, and she refused to release the nobleman's body to them. The result was an interdict over Hildegard's convent—the nuns were refused the sacrament of Communion and not allowed to sing the liturgy or even say their prayers in anything but muffled tones.

While it is difficult for twenty-first-century people to appreciate the impact of such a judgment, in medieval Europe this was in practical terms cutting them off from God's grace. And for the members of a convent, whose very lives were centered on prayer, liturgy, and the sacraments, this was catastrophic. For Hildegard herself, not only did she feel the weight of responsibility for all her spiritual daughters, who found themselves "afflicted with much bitterness,"[12] she must also have felt personal pain at hearing that they were to be denied the ability to sing. For this songwriter par excellence, that must have been a particularly painful blow.

But if her opponents thought such a punishment would bring Hildegard to her knees, they were sorely mistaken. Although she experienced profound sadness because of the interdict, the Sybil of the Rhine remained resolute and did as she had always done: she took action. With letters and visits, she vigorously appealed the decision. Eventually, the ban was lifted, and normalcy returned to the convent. Still, Hildegard had seen for herself how fickle people could be. She was beloved and respected—a living saint in the eyes of some—but still she found herself at the mercy of those who showed her no respect.

The interference didn't stop with her death in 1179. Even then, there were many who started speaking of her as "Saint Hildegard of blessed memory," including Pope Gregory IX. By the time Gregory began his pontificate in 1227, almost half a century had passed since her death at the age of eighty-two, and her legend had grown; some people claimed healing for their bodies and spirits as a result of meeting her while she was alive or even going to her grave. It seemed obvious to many that Hildegard should be declared officially what they already knew her to be—a saint.

But the Church's canonization process had become more stringent and complex under the auspices of a commission appointed to investigate the claim of miracles attributed to any would-be saint. At least two documented miracles were needed to move forward with the canonization process. Though the Church demanded supernatural backing, as it were, a divine reference supporting a candidate's cause, they seemed to disregard the ongoing "miraculous" impact of the saint on both the Church and the world. In any case, it was more difficult to work through the process than it previously had been—or that's what's claimed when the issue of Hildegard's canonization is brought up. The pope himself supported her cause, asserting that the Church "ought now to exalt her on earth whom the Lord has honored in the heavens" and further noting that "something with such obvious proof should not be neglected."[13] It must not have been so "obvious" to the special commission, however, for they failed to find sufficient evidence of legitimate miracles attributed to her. The canonization process died in committee.

Even more interesting is the fact that when a second canonization protocol was initiated a few years later, the findings appear never to have reached Rome at all. It's been suggested that the leaders in Mainz, the diocese of Hildegard's spiritual home, may have chosen to abandon the case. It doesn't take a conspiracy theorist to conjecture that old resentments against the strong-willed woman might still have been playing themselves out. To the claim that the canonization process itself had become so difficult to work through with any degree of success, one has only to look at Francis of Assisi, who lived during the same period and who was officially declared a saint within three years of his death, or Clare of Assisi, whose influence with those in power was similar to Hildegard's and who made it through the canonization process with ease. These both were seen as living saints before their deaths—but so was Hildegard.

DEALING WITH DANGER

Perhaps like other strong women before and after her, there was an inherent bias against lifting Hildegard up as a model. Like Mary Magdalene, Hildegard had proclaimed God's word to the male hierarchy of Church and empire, becoming an apostle to the apostles. She made many friends along the way, but she also made some enemies, who probably felt threatened by this woman who, despite her statements about the fragility of women, showed herself to be anything but fragile. For Hildegard, men and women were together precious in the eyes of God, and all were linked not only with one another but with all the created order in an ecology grounded in divine love. In this way, there is much of the psalmist in Hildegard, with her rich imagery of the Divine calling all who hear to join in a chorus of praise and worship.

Today, as in her own time, people respond to Hildegard's lyrical descriptions, finding their imaginations stirred by phrases such as, "I awaken all to life with every wind of the air,"[14] and again from *O Virtus Sapientie*, "Power of Wisdom, circling all things, comprehending all things, on one path, which has life."[15] Truly,

Hildegard's medium of music served as a message of reverence and intimacy with the Divine. For those with ears to hear, the voice of God inhabited her expressions and utterances. For those tone-deaf to God's harmony, her compositions were a cacophony.

In the end, it didn't matter. For reasons of both envy and neglect, Hildegard of Bingen would never be officially declared a saint. But for countless believers and seekers through the centuries the music of her life has continued to resound and inspire, and Saint Hildegard of blessed memory remains to this day a conduit of God's light and life.

For Reflection

1. Music was such an important part of Hildegard's worship and life. How does music enter into your own experience of God?

2. Hildegard had strong feelings about decisions being made without consulting the person involved. Have you ever experienced a sense of powerlessness while others made important decisions for you? How does Hildegard's response offer you inspiration?

3. What could Hildegard's concept of "greenness" mean for our society today?

For Further Reading

Atherton, Mark, trans. *Hildegard of Bingen: Selected Writings.* New York: Penguin, 2001.

Boyce-Tillman, June. *The Creative Spirit: Harmonious Living with Hildegard of Bingen.* New York: Morehouse, 2001.

Flanagan, Sabina. *Hildegard of Bingen: A Visionary Life.* 2nd ed. New York: Routledge, 1998.

Hamilton, Lisa B. *Wisdom from the Middle Ages for Middle-Aged Women.* New York: Morehouse, 2007.

Hart, Columba, and Jane Bishop, trans. *Hildegard of Bingen: Scivias.* Mahwah, NJ: Paulist Press, 1990.

For a discography of Hildegard's music, go to www.medieval.org/emfaq/composers/hildegard.html.

6
THOMAS CRANMER
The Reformer

We do not presume to come to this thy table,
O Merciful Lord, trusting in our own righteous-
ness, but in thy manifold and great mercies.
—THE BOOK OF COMMON PRAYER

The sixteenth-century Reformation—the European movement that established Protestantism as a branch of the
Christian family of churches—produced a fascinating cast of
characters. Depending on your vantage point, there were heroes
and villains, all of remarkable stature. Although none were
knights clad in shining armor, they were warriors of a different
kind, fighting for what they saw as true faith against dogmas and
practices that they understood to be heresy. They were convinced
of the rightness of their respective causes, and they believed their
struggles were about more than life or death—they were about
eternal salvation or damnation. Their names are legendary:
Martin Luther, John Calvin, Peter Zwingli, Ignatius Loyola …
and Thomas Cranmer.

His influence on religion, politics, and even the English language itself was incomparable, yet Thomas Cranmer never seemed to be marked as one of the major players of the Reformation. Separated from the rest of Europe by the English Channel, the England of the Tudor monarchs seemed worlds away. The substantial changes transforming the continent made their way to England too, but on those shores they seemed to take a different direction. The church there would be neither Catholic nor Protestant but, reflecting its own unique context, thoroughly English—or Anglican. And the first architect of this new structure was neither as colorful as Luther nor as decisive as Calvin. In a time when others were lifted up as heroes, there was little of the heroic to find in Cranmer. Some of his actions in loyalty to the king were distasteful, and when pressured, he recanted all the good he had initiated. Yet with his last words, at his execution, Thomas Cranmer's courage and his story became the stuff of legend.

THE KING'S MAN

There was little that was noteworthy about Cranmer when he first came to the attention of the king. Born in 1489 in Nottinghamshire, he was no aristocrat, and his early years at the then-new and undistinguished Jesus College at Cambridge University were unimpressive. He displayed a greater aptitude for scholarship as he pursued his master's and doctorate degrees, with a clear inclination toward humanism and its poster child, Erasmus. Although he was on his way to becoming a priest, he married a woman named Joan, thereby losing his academic fellowship and the possibility of an ordained life. But when Joan died during childbirth, Cranmer resumed his path and received Holy Orders and shortly thereafter a doctorate of divinity. That early detour from the expected path was a preview of things to come. At that point, however, Cranmer took on minor roles in diplomacy before his life took a radical turn with the situation of the king's "privy matter."

Henry VIII would go down in history as one of England's most famous—and infamous—monarchs. But in 1529, he was simply a very frustrated and somewhat desperate man. Like Cranmer, Henry's early life did not seem directed to greatness, for it was his older brother, Arthur, who was destined to be king. Arthur died, however, leaving Henry to inherit the throne. Arthur also left behind a wife, Catherine of Aragon, to whom Henry was now betrothed against his protests that the Hebrew scriptures' book of Leviticus prohibited a man marrying his deceased brother's widow. A series of miscarriages and the birth of only one child, a daughter Mary—not a son and heir—seemed to Henry's medieval mind to confirm his fears about God's displeasure with his marriage. Henry asked the pope to annul the marriage, thereby releasing Henry to marry a woman who would produce a royal heir. Henry's request wasn't uncommon in that period, but it was complicated by the fact that Catherine's nephew was Charles V, the Holy Roman emperor. Out of loyalty to his aunt, Charles pressured the pope to refuse the annulment. Henry was in a stalemate.

Enter Thomas Cranmer. The annulment case had been given by Henry to his chief advisor, Cardinal Wolsey, who took action by seeking the counsel of university scholars. Cranmer was part of that group. His thoughts on the king's "privy matter" intrigued Wolsey. Cranmer went one step beyond what Wolsey himself had done by suggesting that they put aside the legal case in Rome and instead canvas the opinions of university scholars throughout Europe. Not surprisingly, this idea appealed to King Henry. Indeed, Cranmer was added to the research team. Even in this early encounter with royal politics, Cranmer displayed what would be key qualities he would take with him—confidence in sound scholarship and a growing fascination with reformed theology.

TEMPESTUOUS TIMES

When Martin Luther nailed his ninety-five theses on the door of the church in Wittenberg on All Hallow's Eve 1517, he unknowingly unleashed a torrent of change in the Western world. An Augustinian monk, Luther originally sought merely to challenge the inappropriate trafficking of indulgences and other abuses he saw in the Roman Catholic Church. Instead, an intractable Church hierarchy unwilling to negotiate with critics like Luther, a rising nationalistic spirit throughout Europe, and an increased accessibility to knowledge of all kinds combined to give birth to the epochal period that would become known as the Reformation. Luther, the once-faithful son of the Roman Church, when backed into a corner, retaliated with more vehement arguments and more radical alternatives. "Here I stand," he boldly proclaimed at the Diet, or assembly, of Worms.

And yet it would not be long before reformers more vehement and more radical broke with Luther. The "wild boar in the vineyard," as the pope described Luther, was a pussycat compared to some who demanded he had not gone far enough with his views on baptism, Communion, and even the interpretation of the scriptures. Some, like the Frenchman John Calvin, would focus on God's sovereignty to the point that it was not enough to speak of justification by faith, for no one could even come to faith if that person were not predestined from before time to be part of the community of the elect.

And from Rome's side, to combat this Protestant revolution, came a new religious order with almost military emphasis on discipline and loyalty, a group founded by Ignatius Loyola and known as the Society of Jesus—the Jesuits. All this was occurring on the Continent in the first half of the sixteenth century, and across the Channel in England, Thomas Cranmer took notice.

As an emissary of the king, Cranmer began to travel, encountering first the Swiss reformers who followed in Zwingli's tradition, and eventually the emperor himself, Charles V. During this time, Cranmer married again, an indication of how far this priest had gone down the road toward reformed ideals. He kept the marriage secret, though—a sign of his cautious spirit and tendency to take steps in moderation. For the foreseeable future, Mrs. Cranmer and the children the couple eventually had would live on the Continent, away from prying eyes in England.

Right in the middle of his mission with Charles V, Cranmer received a summons to return home and take up his new duties as the archbishop of Canterbury. How ironic that the secretly married Cranmer received his appointment in 1532, largely through the influence of the family of Anne Boleyn, with whom Henry VIII had become involved and, following quiet word of her pregnancy, would secretly wed. The annulment proceedings with Catherine now took on a more desperate quality, and still Pope Clement VII remained unmovable. Within a few months, now-Archbishop Cranmer pronounced Henry's marriage to Catherine to be nullified, publicly validated his marriage to Anne, and then baptized and even stood as godfather to Henry and Anne's daughter, Elizabeth.

What happened in the months and years that followed must have seemed like a whirlwind of events. For all his impressive rise in the political arena, Cranmer had to take a backseat to Thomas Cromwell, who as vice-regent acted as the king's main agent for spiritual matters. It must have been both bewildering and exhausting to experience the back-and-forth changes that occurred in these years, as various reforms were set in motion, then reversed, and then initiated again. Henry's own life took on a surreal, chaotic quality. When Anne Boleyn failed to give Henry the son and heir he so desperately sought, she who was once described by Catherine of Aragon as "the scandal of Christendom" found herself convicted of adultery and even witchcraft, and met her end by beheading. She was followed by Jane Seymour, who gave Henry a son, though Edward proved to be a sickly child, and Jane herself died soon after childbirth. Then there was Anne of Cleves, whom Henry divorced in an embarrassing situation that resulted in Cromwell's own execution. Then came Catherine Howard, who was executed upon exposure of her extramarital affairs, followed by Katharine Parr, who (amazingly) outlived Henry. Amidst all the dramas of royal marital woes on the one hand and back-and-forth reforms on the other hand, Cranmer remained the king's man, not out of cowardice but rather personal loyalty to the monarch. When Henry died, Cranmer grew a long beard as a sign of mourning—but also a sign of his now fully transparent reformed faith.

COMMON PRAYER

During the brief reign of Henry's son, the young Edward VI, Cranmer oversaw the creation and publication of one of the most influential pieces of literature in the English language, the Book of Common Prayer. Initially published in 1549 and then revised in 1552, this was the first comprehensive collection of materials for worship in the English language. Cranmer had earlier published his worship services known as the Exhortation and Litany, which made their way into the Prayer Book, as did the later ordination services for bishops, priests, and deacons. There would be further slight revisions in the years following Cranmer's death, culminating in the Elizabethan book of 1662, still the authorized Prayer Book in England today and the foundation for Anglican prayer books throughout the world. But it is Cranmer who started it all.

Three things are particularly noteworthy about the Prayer Book. First, it showed Cranmer's concern to wed reformed ideas to the basic structures of Church worship. While there would be ongoing battles in the years ahead over specific issues like vestments or liturgical accoutrements, the sometimes violent excesses and departures from tradition found on the Continent were ameliorated by Cranmer's careful moderation. There would be criticism from extremists on both sides—those who thought he had gone too far in his reforms and those who thought he had not gone far enough—about how far Cranmer had gone with the Prayer Book, but it allowed England to retain its catholic tradition of worship and sacraments while incorporating elements of the reformed faith that had become so important to him. The second thing to note is that thanks to Cranmer, the Reformation in England would be marked by common prayer, not necessarily common thought. This seed would not fully blossom until the reign of Henry's daughter, Elizabeth I, who famously would say that she had no desire to "make windows into men's souls."[1] How many sectarian movements then and now have demanded group-think—that all "true believers" subscribe to a certain set of doc-trines and practices? The history of religious movements, particularly some of the branches of the Reformation, has been marked by division and break-offs each time members disagree with one another. But the genius of the seed that Cranmer planted, and that came to full bloom under Elizabeth, is that communion and community do not have to be based on agree-ment on every theological point.

The third noteworthy thing about the Prayer Book is what it accomplished on the literary level. Along with Shakespeare's works and the King James Bible, the Book of Common Prayer helped reinvent the English language, giving it both a breadth and a profound depth that had not previously been explored. It was not simply the vocabulary, but the cadence and rhythm of the writing that made it both exquisite and memorable. Grounded in Holy Scripture, inheriting forms and structures from Roman and Lutheran liturgies, Cranmer went to a new level altogether in what he produced, opening with a preface that explains so clearly and yet so beautifully why such a work was needed and how its creation could be justified: "There was never any thing by the wit of man so well devised or so surely established, which (in continuance of time) hath not been corrupted." It is almost possible to hear echoes of this acknowledgement of the need for change and ongoing development in the Declaration of Independence, as well as in the provision for amendments in the Constitution of the United States. In this same preface, Cranmer set out the goals of public worship in a language "understanded by the people" and in a book shared by clergy and laypeople alike, saying that the ordained ministers could be "stirred up to godliness themselves" and that the people could be "more inflamed with the love of true religion."

Elsewhere in the Prayer Book, Cranmer offered a more disciplined and respectful approach to the complexities of the Bible than some of his contemporaries who instead resorted to a kind of proof-texting—the practice of choosing out-of-context quotations from the Bible to prove a point you've already decided is correct. The scriptures, Cranmer maintained, were like meat, to be chewed on and slowly digested, not the sixteenth-century equivalent of cotton candy, to be swallowed whole and found to be without substance. As he put it in one of his prayers, Christians are called to "read, mark, learn, and inwardly digest"[2] the scriptures. And while joining the Continental reformers in their concern for sin and redemption, Cranmer also noted in his prayer for Ash Wednesday, the beginning of the penitential season of Lent that precedes Easter, God's deep love for humankind, rooted in creation: "Thou hatest nothing that thou hast made, and dost forgive the sins of all them that be penitent."

While there were opponents who objected to Cranmer's theology, it was impossible to criticize his skilled use of language to raise worshippers to the realm of the Divine. The formal Latin used in worship had found a worthy successor. English had become a more profound and poetic means of expression.

In the period that followed the publication of the Book of Common Prayer, Cranmer initiated further reforms to the Church, through publication of English Canon Law and the Forty-Two Articles of Religion (eventually downsized to thirty-nine). In all this, Cranmer moved in a step-by-step process, believing moderate change more effective than revolution. This moderate seed that Cranmer planted would grow and blossom in the days of Elizabeth, with theologian Richard Hooker speaking of a "middle way" between the excesses of reactionary Rome on the one hand and radical Protestantism on the other. Cranmer started things down that road of moderation, hoping that England could avoid some of the violence he saw occurring elsewhere. Alas, he was not wholly successful.

As it became obvious that young King Edward was dying, there was a scrambling around him as supporters of Lady Jane Grey, the king's cousin and a Protestant, worked hard to gain the king's backing for her to succeed him. According to the rules of succession, the crown was due to go to Mary, daughter of Henry and Catherine of Aragon, and a staunch Roman Catholic. Edward made his will and in it disregarded the Succession Act and instead named Jane as his heir. Cranmer tried to see Edward alone but was unable to do so, as other counselors remained in the room while Edward made his decision clear to his archbishop. Reluctantly or otherwise, the loyal Cranmer supported Edward's choice—and thereby sealed his own doom. For soon after Edward's death, it was Mary, not Jane, who came to the throne. Despite Edward's wishes, despite the fact that Mary represented a return to Rome, the fact remained that she was the firstborn child of Henry and her claim to succession was far stronger than that of Jane.

DEALING WITH DANGER

Despite his seemingly quiet nature, Thomas Cranmer's entire adult life was marked by controversy and revolution. After all, it was he who provided King Henry with the ecclesiastical means for divorcing Catherine of Aragon and breaking ties with the

Church of Rome. It was Cranmer who made sweeping changes to the way Christians in England worshipped and understood their faith. The move from Latin to English in the liturgy, the dissolution of the monasteries, the removal of mandatory celibacy for clergy, the naming of the monarch and not the pope as supreme head of the Church of England—these were sweeping changes that left most people stunned ... and some leaders, like Mary, furious.

While no immediate action was taken against him—he was even able to bury Edward according to the Prayer Book service—Cranmer watched as reformed clergy throughout the Church were removed. It all came to his doorstep when he publicly dismissed rumors that he had allowed the Roman Mass to be said in Canterbury Cathedral. He did no such thing, Cranmer asserted, and moreover added that "all the doctrine and religion, by our said sovereign lord king Edward VI is more pure and according to God's word, than any that hath been used in England these thousand years."[3] These were not simply fighting words; they were a death sentence, as Cranmer was arrested for treason and imprisoned in the Tower of London. It was 1553, twenty years after he had become archbishop of Canterbury.

Cranmer watched as his colleagues and fellow bishops Hugh Latimer and Nicholas Ridley were found guilty of treason and burned at the stake, a preview of what he himself would face. Although he smuggled a letter out to a friend on the European continent praying that "God may grant that we may endure to the end,"[4] he was soon caving in under extreme pressure from his papal interrogator. Having prepared himself for a reasonable and serious debate on the sacrament of Eucharist, or Holy Communion, Cranmer instead was pounded relentlessly by the skilled prosecutor with carefully crafted questions that could only result in damning self-incriminations. Cranmer was devastated. He wrote Queen Mary herself, offering a defense for all he had done to bring about needed reforms in England, which wouldn't have been possible without a break with Rome. The letter gained him nothing. He was again put before an assembly and first clad, then mockingly stripped of every vestment and liturgical accoutrement. When faced with various recantations to sign, Cranmer agreed to acknowledge the pope's authority in England, but only "so far as God's laws and the laws and customs of the realm will permit."[5] None of his first four so-called recantations were really substantive. Cranmer knew it, and so did his opponents. Whatever happened next—whatever torture, brainwashing, or promises that ensued—Cranmer finally broke and signed the fifth and the final recantations. In these, he repudiated all the reforming ideals he had worked so hard to fulfill in his life and ministry. The final recantation does not even reflect Cranmer's writing style; it clearly was written under extreme duress. He was a broken man.

It was then that his enemies made a fateful mistake. Believing him to be without strength, they foisted one more humiliation upon him, demanding that he make a public statement of recantation in order to be a lesson to all those who looked on. They even prepared the phrasing and had Cranmer write the statement out ahead of time. All looked in order, and as the lamentable prisoner stood in the pulpit on the day of his execution, opening with a prayer, calling for obedience to the monarch, he proceeded to recite his written recantation. Suddenly, though, Cranmer veered off the script and surprised all who heard him, recanting all his previous recantations "which I have written or signed with my hand since my degradation."[6] Then, in a poetic flourish, he proclaimed, "And forasmuch as my hand hath offended, writing contrary to my heart, my hand shall first be punished, for when I come to the fire, it shall be first burned."[7] The crowd was stunned, his enemies' advantages all undone, as Cranmer continued, declaring his opposition to the pope before being removed from the pulpit. Later, at the place of execution, Cranmer proved himself to be true to his word, extending his hand and reiterating his desire that it should be the first part of him to be burned.

Queen Mary's forces won the day with the return of the pre-Reformation rites and ways and executed enough Protestants that she gained the awful nickname of "Bloody Mary." By the time Elizabeth came to the throne, the people of England were tired of bloodshed and ready to embrace both peace and peace of mind. By offering reform done in moderation, Elizabeth gave the people a church and a realm in which they could agree to disagree in private while joining in common prayer in public. It was a gift she inherited from her father's and half-brother's archbishop of Canterbury. Thomas Cranmer was no Luther or Calvin, but he didn't have to be. There have been many Christian martyrs before and since who displayed a far greater boldness and heroism in the face of death. Cranmer, on the other hand, far from being bigger than life, was an altogether human figure who appeared to be at war with himself. He was quiet and unassuming, yet audacious in much of his thinking. He was studious and cautious, yet surprising in many of his decisions. He was a staunch believer in hierarchical authority and totally loyal to the king, yet his Prayer Book brought a kind of equality to all who now could share truly common prayer. He was afraid and gave in to his fears, and yet in the end rose above those fears to reach out to heaven's gate. Jesus's parables often had as their protagonists surprising characters like good Samaritans and prodigal sons. And the first followers of Jesus were hardly impressive characters or obvious leaders. In many ways, Thomas Cranmer, for all his internal complexities and apparent contradictions, was an apt successor to such characters. Loving God and wanting above all else to open wider the way of salvation for all God's people, Cranmer initiated reforms that would last. And for the world of the twenty-first century, Thomas Cranmer's greatest gift might well be the reminder that great passion can indeed be wrapped in the garments of moderation.

For Reflection

1. Though Cranmer was a man of strong conviction, he sought the moderate, middle way. Far from being the way of easy compromise, his way of moderation was challenged and challenging. When has your faith journey compelled you to look for a middle way?

2. Cranmer recanted, and then recanted his earlier recantation. Have there been times when you realized you had made a mistake and needed to change your course?

3. The Anglican way that Cranmer initiated asserted that common prayer, not common agreement, is what joins Christians together. Do you know some Christians with whom you disagree on significant issues, yet still feel comfortable praying with them?

For Further Reading

Barbee, C. Frederick, and Paul F. M. Zahl, eds. *The Collects of Thomas Cranmer.* Grand Rapids: Eerdmans, 2006.

Brooks, Peter Newman. *Cranmer in Context: Documents from the English Reformation.* Minneapolis: Fortress, 1989.

MacCulloch, Diarmaid. *Thomas Cranmer: A Life.* New Haven, CT: Yale University Press, 1998.

✞

7

SOJOURNER TRUTH

The Liberator

I cannot read a book, but I can read the people.
—SOJOURNER TRUTH

There were few people who could match Sojourner Truth, the uneducated former slave turned abolitionist, when it came to working a crowd. She was tall, tough, and tenacious, thoroughly committed to the cause of freedom and equality. Her ever-present cane was the consequence of injuries she received when she was beaten to within an inch of her life—yet still she pressed on. During an attempt to integrate streetcars in the nation's capital, she was sorely hurt, her shoulder dislocated—yet still she pressed on. She made many enemies, but even more friends and allies and grateful admirers. Frederick Douglass once described her as "a strange compound of wit and wisdom, of wild enthusiasm and flint-like common sense."[1] Harriett Beecher Stowe, author of *Uncle Tom's Cabin*, called her the "Libyan Sybil,"[2] a reference to the female oracles of ancient Greece, whose name "Sybil" literally means "prophet."

What was it that fueled this remarkable individual, that enabled her to hold her own with preachers and presidents and accomplish all that she did against impossible odds? Sojourner Truth was quick to answer, "You read books; I talk to God."[3] Her spiritual conversion, her faith, and her determination combined to make her a formidable force, whether fighting against slavery or pushing for women's rights. A divided country around her would learn that it was no match for "the power of a nation"[4] that was within God's sojourner.

A Slave's Life

She was born a slave. Her parents, James and Betsey, were slaves, as were her brothers and sisters, some of whom she never even met, as her older siblings were sold and forever gone while she was still young. But her mother, "Mau-Mau Bett," made sure that she would not forget them by telling her stories about them and reminding her of their names. Names were important, for they formed connections across years and across miles. Her own given name was Isabella, and she was born into slavery as the property of a Dutchman named Charles Ardinburgh. Years later she dictated her experiences in a book appropriately called the *Narrative of Sojourner Truth: A Northern Slave*, one of the most important documents ever written about the harsh realities of slavery. She spoke of being whipped with "a bundle of rods, prepared in the embers, and bound together with cords"[5] while owned by one family, and then alluded to even worse, unspeakable sufferings at the hands of another family. But what seems to have been most difficult was not the physical abuse but the lack of personal dignity or human identity as a piece of property, a thing that can be bought and sold. Isabelle was reminded again and again that freedom was not hers. When she fell in love with Robert, who was owned by another slave master, she learned how cruel the system could be. Robert's owner did not want his slave procreating with someone else's "property," since any progeny would belong to that other master, and there was no profit for him, so the man was beaten and hauled back, bound, to his owner's home, never to see Isabella again. She was forced instead to marry an old slave who belonged to her owner. Her son, Peter, was illegally sold to someone in Alabama, and she had to fight through the courts to retrieve him. For Isabella, freedom was a dream that seemed far outside her grasp.

The so-called "peculiar institution" of slavery, accepted by many otherwise benign and even religious persons, was, to Isabella, an inherently flawed, inherently sinful system "diametrically opposed to the religion of Jesus."[6] When her slave owner, Mr. Dumont, promised to free Isabella a year before the proposed date of emancipation in New York State and then reneged on his promise, she took matters into her own hands. Finishing the season's work in order to be true to her own sense of obligation, Isabella escaped before dawn with her infant daughter. "I did not run off, for I thought that wicked, but I walked off, believing that to be all right."[7] Like Pharoah in the narrative of Jewish slavery in the Hebrew scriptures, Dumont chased after her and found her at the home of a kind couple who welcomed Isabella and even paid a year's debt to Dumont to release her from obligations to him. The couple then took her in, insisting she call them by their first names, Isaac and Maria, a far cry from the "master" and "mistress" to which Isabella was accustomed. They were like angels opening up a new world to her.

GOD'S BREATH

During her trials and tribulations, Isabella had always followed her mother's advice and prayed, usually out loud and outside, because she thought God would better hear her that way. But during her time with Isaac and Maria, Isabella grew lax in prayer, no longer feeling the desperate need that had drawn her heart to God in the past. It was during this time when things were going so well, when she seemed to need God less, that she had a surprising spiritual experience that transformed her life.

One day, Mr. Dumont appeared at her door, just as Isabella had dreamed the night before. From her dream, she believed that she was to return with him to her former state as his slave, much to Isaac's and Maria's astonishment. Even as she faced her former master, God was revealed to her "with all the suddenness of a flash of lightning," filling her with the awareness that there "was no place where God was not." It was an overwhelming moment—not only was she cognizant of just how big God is, she also became aware of her own failings and her fears that she had insulted God with her sins. She wondered if she would be "stricken from existence, swallowed up" by the fire that is God. In awe of what she called the "terror and dread" of the Divine presence, she wished for a mediator, a "friend to stand between herself and an insulted deity."[8] The next moment, she somehow knew that she was not alone, that she did indeed have such a friend. But who was this unfamiliar ally? Surely not one of the companions around her; this much she knew. "Who are you?" Isabella asked over and over, "in one deep prayer that this heavenly personage might be revealed to her and remain with her." When the answer finally came, it both surprised her and seemed like something she had known all along: "It is Jesus," she heard a voice say. "Yes," she responded, "it is Jesus."[9]

She later spoke of this spiritual awakening as "God's breath" that had come and filled her and made her a new person. For the next several years, she grew in her spiritual awareness as well as in her giftedness as a preacher. This period also included spiritual extremes, as she became part of a sectarian group in New York City, led by a cult-like leader called Matthias, who affirmed her gifts even as he led the group in increasingly bizarre behavior. Isabella learned much in this period about both the love of God and the hypocrisy of some who claimed to follow God, as the group drained her hard-earned savings and stained her reputation. When she finally left the city in 1843, she completed what was begun when she first encountered God's breath. She changed her name to Sojourner Truth. "The Spirit calls me," she said, "and I must go."[10]

AIN'T I A WOMAN?

The former Isabella, now Sojourner, did indeed go ... and encountered some notable figures along the way, all of whom were astonished by this illiterate yet "miraculous" extemporaneous speaker. The abolitionist William Lloyd Garrison was so impressed that he published her *Narrative*. And Frederick Douglass acknowledged her gifts and influence, though he treated her with condescension because of her lack of education and cultural breeding. She was for Douglass both an embarrassment and an amazing colleague. She even conversed with President Abraham Lincoln.

But it was not the great and important who most benefitted from Sojourner's gift of proclamation. It was the countless slaves and other underdogs who looked to her to be their voice and share her story—which was their story, as well. Her connections with pacifist, abolitionist, sectarian movements led her to value nonviolence, though she also was willing to recruit black troops for the Union's cause, believing that defeating the evil of slavery was worth the ultimate sacrifice. Her own grandson enlisted in the Fifty-Fourth Massachusetts Regiment. With the close of the Civil War, Sojourner continued to speak and work on behalf of freed slaves, knowing that the battle for true freedom and equality was not won with the surrender of Lee to Grant at Appomattox.

Although she bought a house near Battle Creek, Michigan, Sojourner hardly slowed down after the Civil War. She traveled extensively, speaking about everything from prison reform to capital punishment, but her first priority remained equal rights for African Americans. And though her claim to have written a song for the First Michigan Black Regiment titled "The Valiant Soldiers" has been disputed, she could indeed rightly claim to be one of the first "Freedom Riders"—a century before Rosa Parks and the twentieth-century civil rights movement—when she rode in Washington, D.C., streetcars in an attempt to desegregate them.

Her former master, Mr. Dumont, had realized even before the war that slavery was "the wickedest thing in the world, the greatest curse the earth has ever felt."[11] But there were many more who did not share this realization, even after the war. Beginning in 1870, Sojourner began a long, difficult, and ultimately unsuccessful fight to obtain federal land grants for former slaves. She campaigned for the cause and paid dearly for it, developing painful ulcers on her legs and even losing her young grandson, who died while traveling with her. Eventually, freed slaves made their way out West on their own, but that exodus came almost a decade after Sojourner first fought for federal support for them to do so.

The other cause to which Sojourner gave her energy was equal rights for women. Lucretia Mott and Susan B. Anthony, early champions in the women's movement, were among those who called her colleague and friend. Indeed, Sojourner's most famous speech, given at the Ohio Woman's Rights Convention in 1851, was titled "Ain't I a Woman?" She challenged all who listened, "I have as much muscle as any man, and can do as much work as any man." It was hard to debate the six-foot-plus wiry, muscled woman on the level of strength and endurance. In fact, in one of her more humorous—and politically incorrect— moments, in response to a heckler's challenge that Sojourner wasn't a woman at all, but a man in disguise, she simply lifted her blouse, revealing her breasts. And to any who might suggest that men were superior to women in intellect, she countered in "Ain't I a Woman?" by stating, "As for intellect, all I can say is, if a woman have a pint, and a man a quart, why can't she have her little pint full?" Sojourner went to the heart of the matter, acknowledging how threatened white men must feel—"the poor slave is on him, the woman is coming on him"—but also confirming that they had better get used to it. This would not only be true for the nation, but for the Church, as she was quick to challenge those who used the fact that Christ was not a woman to support less-than-equal rights for women. It would be many decades before women could be ordained as ministers, priests, and bishops, but Sojourner seemed to pave the way for it, as she reminded any who would listen that although Christ was indeed a man, he came "from God and a woman!"[12]

DEALING WITH DANGER

When Isabella became Sojourner Truth, she understood her mission to be one of "lecturing" as she called it, "testifying to the hope that was in her."[13] There were other advocates for abolition and women's rights, but it was her passionate faith that made Sojourner such an unforgettable, unstoppable force. It also at times made her a threat to the establishment, both secular and religious. She had little compunction about standing up to powers and authorities, whether in challenging slavery or fighting for full and equal rights for women. And though born a slave, Sojourner displayed a complete lack of intimidation in the presence of public luminaries. Indeed, her well of common sense was deep and provided her with internal resources that were more than a match for the so-called sophistication she encountered. Illiterate, she needed others to read her beloved scriptures aloud to her but preferred for her readers to be children. Adults, she complained, would interject their own opinions, their own commentary, which would get in the way of her own interpretation and thereby "tried her feelings exceedingly."[14] Children, on the other hand, would simply read what was written, allowing Sojourner to "compare the teachings of the Bible with the witness within her."[15] As she engaged in such direct engagement with the scriptures, she realized that even as her adult readers interposed their own voice into the divine conversation, so too did the original recorders of the scriptures. As in so many things, without knowing it, Sojourner was ahead of her time in what would later become known as biblical criticism (though she would never have phrased it that way). Indeed, for one who was a firm believer, Sojourner was blessed to have a critic's ability to see nonsense. When confronted by a sectarian group about waiting for the New Jerusalem, she challenged them to make a difference in the here and now. When she witnessed their ecstatic rituals, she commented that in the state they were in, "the Lord might come and move all through the camp" without their even knowing it.[16]

The God of the Bible, Sojourner believed, was with us right here, right now, calling us to make a difference in our world and not simply wait for a new world to come. She rejoiced when a group of freed slaves and other refugees did finally make their way west well after the Civil War. In what was to be her last sojourn, she herself spent a year both living among these "Exodusters" and seeking support from various churches on their behalf. What she saw them doing, what she herself tried to do for them, was for Sojourner simply faith in action. This was true of all her advocacy work, all her political activism. Sojourner was committed to trusting God. As William Lloyd Garrison, who wrote the preface to the 1850 edition of her *Narrative*, said of her, Sojourner kept her eyes forever fixed on Jesus, through all the trials and struggles she encountered. This is why she was able to march into the fray with her head held high, facing outright hostility from those who disapproved of her cries for equal rights for African Americans and women, and condescension from those who made too much of her illiteracy and not enough of her message. She knew that Jesus, who stood by her when she was most greatly in need, would stand with her as she helped to meet the needs of the world around her.

Although three editions of her *Narrative* were published in her lifetime, soon after her death in 1883 the book went out of print, only to receive new life when the civil rights movement of the

1960s called for African American histories. Even in those intervening years, Sojourner was honored in many ways: a painting of her meeting with Abraham Lincoln was commissioned, and historical markers were sponsored by the Sojourner Truth Memorial Association. In more recent years, she has been the subject of a commemorative stamp and even had a NASA Mars probe named "Sojourner" after her. Perhaps most appropriate is the fact that in 2008, this former slave who originally had no last name but that of her owner, who even after her emancipation was treated as a second-class citizen, became the first African American woman honored with a bust in the United States Capitol. She had lived out her faith in the midst of many who were intimidated by a strong black woman who refused to be bound by others' preconceptions of how things were supposed to be. But Sojourner always looked to what things could be, by God's grace and sheer perseverance.

For Reflection

1. There was nothing pretentious about Sojourner Truth. She was always direct, always honest in her dealings with people. Whom do you go to when you need forthright, honest feedback? Would others come to you for the same, and if not, why not?

2. How did Sojourner pave the way for other prophets who would fight for full and equal rights for all? Where do we still see a need for such prophets?

3. Sojourner spoke of "God's breath" filling her and making her a new person. When have you experienced "God's breath," in you or in someone you know?

For Further Reading

Painter, Nell Irvin. *Sojourner Truth: A Life, A Symbol.* New York: W. W. Norton, 1997.

Stetson, Erlene, and Linda David. *Glorying in Tribulation: The Lifework of Sojourner Truth.* East Lansing, MI: Michigan State University Press, 1994.

Washington, Margaret, ed. *Narrative of Sojourner Truth.* New York: Vintage, 1993.

For the official Sojourner Truth Institute website, go to www.sojournertruth.org.

8
DOROTHY DAY
The Activist

I wanted the abundant life, but I did not have
the slightest idea how to find it.
—DOROTHY DAY, *THE LONG LONELINESS*

I f ever there was an unlikely Christian hero, it was Dorothy Day.
Born at the turn of the twentieth century, as a young adult she
had little love for the Roman Catholic Church of her time, and
considering the life she lived, the feeling was probably mutual.
However, although she didn't know how to find the abundant life
she sought, through a long and circuitous route that abundant life
found her. When she embraced Christianity, she embraced it with
gusto, immersing herself in the mission and ministry of Jesus to
the poor in the dark days of the Great Depression. And whatever
eyebrows she raised before her conversion, it was nothing compared to what happened afterward!

THE LONG LONELINESS

By the time she actually came into the Church, Dorothy Day had
already experienced an adventurous, controversial life. Born in

Brooklyn in 1897, she grew up in a tenement in Chicago's South Side, experiencing poverty firsthand as her father struggled to find work. Even after he landed a position as a sports editor at a Chicago newspaper, enabling the Day family to move to the much nicer North Side, young Dorothy never forgot what she saw in those early years and would often find herself visiting the neighborhoods she had left. Dropping out of college and moving to New York City, she became part of a circle of artists, writers, and activists—the playwright Eugene O'Neill was included among their number—many of whom were outspoken in their socialist ideals, which Dorothy shared. She lived out her convictions through positions she held first with *The Call*, a daily socialist publication, and later with *The Masses*, which spoke out against American involvement in what would eventually be known as World War I. These publications provoked reaction, as a handful of editors were charged with sedition.

Day's first personal brush with the law came in November 1917, when she was arrested and imprisoned as one of forty women advocating for women's suffrage in front of the White House; she and her companions participated in a hunger strike before they were freed by presidential pardon. Day could have ended up as a leader of a political party, but life took her in a different direction. Along the way, she fell in love with a fellow journalist, became pregnant, and had an abortion, a decision that haunted her. Her novel, *The Eleventh Virgin*, deals with the pain that came from that experience.

Her journey took her back to New York, this time to a small beach cottage on Staten Island, which she bought with money from the sale of movie rights for her novel. There she began a four-year common-law marriage with Forster Batterham, an anarchist strenuously opposed to religion. Their relationship resulted in another pregnancy—nothing less than a miracle to Dorothy—and brought an end to a period of deep longing in her life, which she described in her autobiography, *The Long Loneliness*. But the pregnancy also represented the final nail in the coffin of her relationship with Batterham. By the time Tamar Teresa Day was born in the spring of 1927, Dorothy was a single parent.

But she was also something else by this time: a believer. Along the circuitous route of her faith journey, God somehow had snuck up on her. Little by little, she found herself drawn in by the beauty of liturgical worship and the appeal of spiritual discipline. Even during her time with Eugene O'Neill and the rest of her bohemian friends at the saloon they called "the Hell Hole," Day would find herself in need of the peace and comfort that she found in her early-morning visits to St. Joseph's Church in Greenwich Village.

When Tamar was born, Day made the life-changing decision to baptize her. "I knew I was not going to have her foundering through many years as I had done," Day wrote in *From Union Square to Rome*, "doubting and hesitating, undisciplined and amoral."[1] Dorothy's decision to take the next step and be formally received into the Church herself was a more painful one, for it involved choosing between God and Batterham. As grueling as it was to make, the choice was clear.

Now the crucial question before Dorothy was, how could she reconcile her faith with her social activism? Surely God did not want her to dismiss a lifetime of solidarity with those in need. "I offered up a special prayer," she said later, "a prayer which came with tears and anguish, that some way would open up for me to use what talents I possessed for my fellow workers, the poor."[2]

A door did open—the very next day, in fact. Dorothy met Peter Maurin, a French immigrant and former member of the religious order known as the Christian Brothers, who fully embraced poverty as his spiritual vocation. Twenty years her senior, this twentieth-century St. Francis caught Dorothy's attention and stoked her spiritual imagination. Critiquing both capitalism and Communism, Maurin argued instead for what he termed a "personalist revolution," where each person could make a difference in the here and now, not waiting for the right moment in the abstract future but doing what could and should be done in the present. Maurin was also a master of the one- or two-liner. He had volumes of what he called "easy essays," pithy statements that could be rattled off and remembered easily. Although he didn't come up with this modern quip, Maurin's belief could be summed up with the familiar "If not you, then who? If not now, then when?"

The Church was integral to Maurin's vision, for through it God could reignite in human beings the passion and purpose that had been lost in Western society. Yet the Church had more often than not failed to proclaim in word and deed the message that it alone could. The quotation attributed to Maurin in the 1996 film *Entertaining Angels: The Dorothy Day Story*, says it well: "You know what is wrong with the world? The people who act do not think, and the people who think do not act." Dorothy Day—the journalist, the activist, the Christian—wanted to be a person who did both. And thus was born the *Catholic Worker*.

The penny-a-copy, eight-page tabloid was created out of her own kitchen, and with Maurin's help, Day put together a team that produced and distributed the paper monthly. From the moment the first copies went out on May 1, 1933, people took notice. Within the first several months, the *Catholic Worker* increased from an initial run of 2,500 copies to 100,000 copies per month, and then up to well over 150,000. Through the publication, Day combined her faith with her social convictions, reminding people through her actions that God truly is as close as the closest human being.

Peter Maurin contributed essays that called for a radical hospitality to those in need, often in the form of his "easy essays." In those early years, Peter and Dorothy often did not agree—her socialist experience combined with a dose of pragmatism, while he never swayed from his idealistic "personalist revolution"—but the partnership bore great fruit.

The paper was only one piece in the overall work that was developing. People read about the concept of creating houses of hospitality, where the poor could live in community and be treated with dignity, and soon they were actually showing up on the *Catholic Worker*'s doorstep. The publishing ministry now expanded to include an even more direct sign of Christian activism. This was not an easy shift for Day to make, but she embraced it, much to the frustration of her brother John, sister-in-law Tessa, and the rest of the publishing team, who were utterly committed to promoting the cause but did not always understand this more hands-on approach.

Dorothy, however, was undeterred. Scrounging for whatever money could be found, she secured apartment rentals to help people who had fallen on hard times. It wasn't long before there were three dozen homes of hospitality all across the country, and to these were added farming communes as well. While Peter Maurin had spoken of the possibility of "agricultural universities" where scholars and farmers could together create a self-sustainable community, in real life things didn't work out quite that way, but as rural examples of houses of hospitality, the communes thrived. Somewhere along the way, Dorothy the single mother had become a mother to more people than she could possibly have imagined.

SAINT OR COMMUNIST?

It wasn't long before the Church hierarchy knocked on Day's door, not to applaud her efforts, but to challenge them. At first, they expressed concern about the apparent socialist approach she brought to her work with those in need. Monsignor Edward Gaffney of the Archdiocese of New York insisted she take the word "Catholic" out of the *Catholic Worker*, and then she could do whatever she wanted—she could prove herself, he said, to be a tool of the Communists. But Day challenged the hypocrisy in his argument: "If you feed the poor, you're a saint. If you question why they are poor, you're a Communist. We do both here, but we're neither saints nor Communists!"[3]

She may not have been a Communist, but her words and actions were unabashedly revolutionary. In an article titled "Poverty Is to Care and Not to Care" in the April 1953 issue of the *Catholic Worker*, she wrote, "The class structure is our making and by our consent, not God's, and we must do what we can to change it." But Day's work wasn't grounded in Communism, despite her background. Rather, everything she did was grounded in Christian faith and prayer. Following in the footsteps of her hero, Francis of Assisi, Day was determined to do what Jesus called her to do, no matter what.

Controversy became her constant companion, one she refused to avoid. Wherever she saw injustice or inequality, she saw Jesus being crucified anew. And she didn't just observe this from a safe distance; she insisted on living her life intentionally in the midst of the poverty. She knew that it was not her job to tell people how to live their lives, but instead to assure them that God loved them. Intentionally or otherwise, Day and Maurin had established a "street apostolate," a movement of the laity where they were doing more than sitting in pews or working on the church council. The ever-increasing membership of the Catholic Worker Movement was collectively making a difference in urban and rural settings, and the movement was attracting attention.

It wasn't simply that Day and her team lived among and ministered to the poor. It was the kind of poor she welcomed that resulted in even greater objections from the Church hierarchy. In her houses of hospitality were found prostitutes and drunkards. She must have looked a bit like Jesus as he surrounded himself with tax collectors and "sinners." And like Jesus, she was confronted about this, not only by opponents but even by some of her own workers, especially as they saw the inherent dangers of taking in strangers who might, under the influence of alcohol or mental illness, try to harm themselves or others. Day's answer, however, was always forthright and absolute: "Once they are taken in, they become members of the family. Or rather they were always members of the family. They are our brothers and sisters in Christ."[4]

She stood resolute in this conviction, even when some of these "brothers and sisters" threatened her with violence or when her colleagues threatened to leave. "We cannot love God unless we love each other," she later wrote in her postscript to *The Long Loneliness*, "and to love we must know each other. We are not alone."[5] What is perhaps most remarkable is that she raised her daughter Tamar in the midst of all this.

It was Day's pacifism, however, that brought on the greatest opposition, not in the earliest years of the Catholic Worker, since that was the period between the wars. But with Franco's Civil War in Spain, followed quickly by World War II, pacifism became a major point of contention. With Franco, there were Americans and American Catholics on both sides; Day's neutral position did not go over well with either group. As Hitler ascended to power in Germany, Day helped found the Committee of Catholics to Fight Anti-Semitism in 1939. This lobbyist group tried to lift the immigration quotas for European Jews while also speaking against the anti-Semitic statements of key Catholic figures of that time, especially Father Charles Coughlin, a controversial priest who used his popular radio program to preach an anti-Semitic message.

But even as she opposed what Hitler stood for, Dorothy likewise stood against what she saw as inhumane ways of dealing with such a tyrant. The Allies' indiscriminate bombings resulting in the deaths of countless civilians, as at Dresden, were indefensible to Day. By fighting a monster in this way, she believed Americans were becoming monsters themselves. And with the use of the atomic bomb at Hiroshima and Nagasaki, she insisted that America had crossed a line that she believed to be nothing less than the ultimate blasphemy.

Day's position brought her under the scrutiny of J. Edgar Hoover, director of the FBI. Like the monsignor who once challenged her for her socialist leanings, Hoover had grave concerns about her and her organization. Five hundred pages were devoted to the Catholic Worker file that the FBI drew up, and Hoover went so far as to recommend prosecution of Dorothy Day on the grounds of sedition. He accused her of engaging in activities that suggested she was being used by Communist groups, whether she was aware of it or not. Dorothy had little patience for the Bureau's intimidation tactics and even less for the dissent raised by her own teammates in light of her pacifism. Working for peace, she believed, was not some tangential piece to the "real work" with the poor, as some asserted. Peacemaking went hand in hand with mercy toward those in need. To follow Jesus meant being a person of peace as well as a person of mercy and justice. Anything less than this, Dorothy believed, dishonored God. After all, she argued, people were suffering and dying as much from the effects of war and indiscriminate killing as they were from poverty and sickness.

By Little and by Little

Toward the end of her life, Day rejoiced that so many people joined her in the work that brought her into active engagement with the major social issues of each period of the twentieth century—from the Depression in the thirties and World War II in the forties through civil defense drills in the fifties and civil rights struggles in the sixties. Jim Forest, managing editor of the *Catholic Worker* in Dorothy's later years, noted that her commitment to justice was grounded in her faith and devotional life, in her conviction that the Church cannot sit back and let government alone deal with problems and that the most radical, most revolutionary thing we can do is to seek to find the face of Jesus in one another. Perhaps most interesting was Forest's recognition of the influence of St. Therese of Lisieux, the nineteenth-century French Carmelite nun whose "Little Way" embraced the spiritual power of doing small things rather than mighty works. Day believed that we cannot wait for the future to begin making a difference; change begins right here, right now, even if only through the planting of a seed that will blossom later. She was convinced that although our actions may seem like nothing more than casting a tiny pebble into the water, the implications in the long run are like the ripples the pebble makes.

Often, Dorothy's pebbles created ripples of reaction, as establishment leaders in both society and the Church continued to be threatened by her words and actions. When New York, along with other states, required mandatory civil defense drills in the 1950s, she refused to participate and was jailed several times for up to thirty days at a time because of her refusal. Her civil disobedience originated not from arrogance or lack of patriotism, but from a belief that nuclear weapons as deterrents represented a blasphemous evil that she could not support or tolerate. Arrest and imprisonment were a small price to pay, she believed, for standing up for life.

More arrests and jail sentences followed, for her work in causes that included the civil rights and the Vietnam anti-war movements, but the common denominator in all of this was the need to stand up and be counted rather than remain a silent conspirator. In 1973, at the age of seventy-five, she received her last jail sentence, for her part in a picket line for the United Farm Workers.

Admirers found it easy to look on Dorothy Day as a superhuman force; to detractors, she was an angry rebel. But both assumptions were wrong. She was a flesh-and-blood human being—a romantic on the one hand, who never lost her sense how things should and could be, and a pragmatist on the other, who knew that it took hard work to help make the ideal a reality here on earth.

The words Dorothy Day wrote about St. Therese of Lisieux, the "Little Flower," could easily have been written about herself: "She, the realist, well knew that suffering of body and soul is not lofty and exalted, but mean and cruel.... It was not suffering for itself that she embraced. It was a means to an end."[6] This attitude enabled Day to face hostile words and even more hostile actions, as when Ku Klux Klan members shot at her car when she stood by the people at Koinonia Farm, an interracial community in Georgia, in 1957. Day did not embrace poverty or allow herself to be arrested and imprisoned because she was some kind of religious masochist. Rather, like Therese, her actions stemmed from her confidence that God had loved this world enough to die for it. Therese's dying words were a kind of creed for Dorothy: "Love alone matters." And like another Christian mystic, Catherine of Sienna, Dorothy was able to endure the struggles and sufferings of this life because she believed that "all the way to heaven is heaven."[7]

It is "by little and by little," as she often said, that salvation comes to individuals and to a broken world alike. This is why it was so important to Dorothy to do a little bit of good every day, no matter how inconsequential it might appear, seeing and serving Jesus in everyone she met: the homeless, the imprisoned, the vulnerable, the enemy. Jesus, for her, was "disguised under every type of humanity that treads the earth."[8] Such a sentiment was rarely appreciated and often misinterpreted. When a well-known interviewer asked her if God loves murderers or dictators like Hitler and Stalin, Day chose not to be baited into a political or theological argument, but instead simply responded that God loves all and that we are called to follow God, not give in to our fears.

DEALING WITH DANGER

In so many ways, Dorothy Day was a dangerous woman. She threatened the secular authorities as she worked for peace in the face of war. She threatened the Church hierarchy as she put the powerful teachings of Jesus into action. And when jail sentences and FBI files didn't silence her, and threats from the archdiocese didn't convince her to abandon her hands-on Christianity, those in authority turned to another tactic: domestication. Gradually, opposition to Day and her work gave way to adulation, as people began to put her on a pedestal. *Time* magazine called her a "living saint."[9] But she was no more likely to be swayed by hero worship than by antagonism: "Too much praise makes you feel you must be doing something wrong."[10] As she approached her last days, Day had experienced far too much good and far too much grief in her journey to get caught up in her own press. She had lived long enough to witness the birth of a great-grandchild, and long enough to grieve that child's death in an accident. She had seen the movement she and Peter Maurin began grow and flourish, and she had also seen the hurts and evils of the world continue in new guises. Reading the scriptures alongside Boris Pasternak's great novel *Dr. Zhivago*, staring at the storm clouds rolling in, receiving cards from well-wishers, and praying—always praying—Day left this world still holding on to her lifelong conviction that what really, truly matters is our love for God made evident in intentional care for our fellow human beings. For Dorothy Day, this is what it means to follow Jesus. And this is what she tried to do and, like Jesus, to do it no matter what the cost.

For Reflection

1. The gospel called Dorothy Day to devote her life to the poor and marginalized. Why do you think her work posed a danger to Church authorities?

2. Who are contemporary leaders who minister to the poor or who work for causes such as ending war? In what ways is their work related to the work of Dorothy Day?

3. Dorothy Day sought to live a life of "little works." How can you adopt that philosophy in your own life?

For Further Reading

Coles, Robert. *Dorothy Day: A Radical Devotion*. Cambridge, MA: Da Capo Press, 1989.

Day, Dorothy. *The Long Loneliness*. New York: Harper & Row, 1952.

———. *Selected Writings*. Edited by Robert Ellsberg. Maryknoll, NY: Orbis Books, 2005.

Ellsberg, Robert, ed. *The Duty of Delight: The Diaries of Dorothy Day*. Milwaukee: Marquette University Press, 2008.

Forest, Jim. "The Living Legacy of Dorothy Day." In *Salt of the Earth*. Chicago: Claretian Publications, 1996.

For an inspiring film portrayal of her life, see *Entertaining Angels: The Dorothy Day Story*. DVD. Directed by Michael Rhodes, starring Moira Kelley and Martin Sheen. Clinton, NY: Vision Video, 1996.

9

DIETRICH BONHOEFFER
The Resister

I am most grateful for the people I have met, and I only hope that they never have to grieve about me.

—DEITRICH BONHOEFFER, FINAL LETTER
FROM TEGEL PRISON, 1945

The war's end was within sight. In April 1945, it was clear that Hitler's dream of a "thousand-year reich" was all but finished. Yet even as the days counted down to his own suicide, the dictator ordered one last set of executions for a group of prisoners he particularly despised. Among these was a young German pastor and theologian who once said that whenever Jesus calls us, he always calls us to die. That prisoner may have meant these words to be understood in less literal, more spiritual terms, but he also knew firsthand what it meant to be ready to stand up for, and die for, Jesus. His name was Dietrich Bonhoeffer.

UNWELCOME SACRIFICE

From his earliest days, Bonhoeffer was well prepared for his eventual civil resistance and martyrdom. His family offered him strength, support, and a solid foundation. Born in 1906, Dietrich and his twin sister, Sabine, along with their other six siblings, enjoyed a happy childhood. His father, Karl, was a professor of psychiatry and neurology at the University of Berlin, and his mother, Paula, had earned a teaching degree, so unsurprisingly there was great emphasis on learning, music, and exploration in the household. Their income allowed for servants and for a governess, Kate Horn, who homeschooled the younger children, including Dietrich. Saturday evenings were devoted to music, with Dietrich quickly learning to play piano proficiently. And on those evenings, his father would read aloud literary classics, including Dietrich's favorites, *Pinocchio* and *Uncle Tom's Cabin*. It was a calm and peaceful existence.

That calm was shattered with the coming of World War I. The two oldest Bonhoeffer boys enlisted in the infantry, and a mere two weeks later, Walter Bonhoeffer was fatally wounded. His death rocked the entire family, with their mother withdrawing from the family altogether for a time as she struggled to cope with the loss of her son. As for Dietrich, his brother's death left an indelible impression on the eleven-year-old boy. In that moment, he learned about self-sacrifice as well as the futility of war. There had to be something greater than the disputes and ambitions of human beings, something truly worthy of sacrifice. Inheriting Walter's Bible—and reading it closely—Dietrich began to see a direction for his future. By age fourteen, he had decided that he would grow up to become a theologian. When his brothers teased him about this and even told him that the Church wasn't worth his time, his response was clear and direct: "Then I shall reform it!"[1]

Bonhoeffer later spoke of the years following World War I as "a new epoch of suffering and grief," and of his homeland as "a house of mourning."[2] The Versailles Treaty that marked the formal end of the war brought down upon Germany the wrath and retribution of the rest of the Western world and planted seeds of resentment and injured pride in the Germans themselves. The economic struggles, the hunger and joblessness only added to the heartache of the people. The postwar government was helpless to make a difference, as the so-called Weimar Republic proved itself incapable of tackling the very real problems the people faced. Desperate times led to violence, discontent, and a cry for a return to greatness for Germany. As if on cue, Adolph Hitler arrived on the national scene.

No Cheap Grace

By 1930, the National Socialist Party had been energetically wooing the populace, and their efforts began paying off. In the national elections, the Nazis made considerable gains, and the anti-Jewish sentiment the party espoused was increasing. Fascism was on the rise, and even churches began to fly the Nazi flag. Bonhoeffer grew into adulthood during this period and was one of the first Christians in Germany to see—and publicly address—the dangers inherent in the movement. Throughout the 1920s, following his announcement that he would become a theologian, Dietrich dove into his vocational choice with fervor, displaying both an energy and a depth of commitment to questions of life and death, of good and evil, and doing so in the specific context of life in Nazi Germany.

Bonhoeffer made his way to Tübingen for university studies and immersed himself in the research, reciting texts of Martin Luther from memory and giving special attention to the contemporary work of Swiss theologian Karl Barth, whose writings marked a departure from the liberal scholars of his day. Bonhoeffer's dissertation, *The Communion of Saints*, showed the clear influence of Barth's thinking, while also hinting at the themes that became Bonhoeffer's own.

One of his greatest influences during this period of life was his own grandmother, with whom he lived while in Tübingen. Julia Bonhoeffer legendarily stood up to a group of Nazi SA troops who were blocking the entrance to her favorite shop because the owner was Jewish. Her response, "I buy my butter where I always buy it," as she moved past the guards, was a practical living-out of the principles Bonhoeffer read about in Luther and Barth.

The other crucial piece in Bonhoeffer's personal education was his corresponding work as a pastor, first overseeing a children's Sunday school program in Berlin and later, in his post-university life, as an assistant pastor in Barcelona, Spain, teaching youth and working with a social welfare program. Returning to Germany to write a second thesis, *Act and Being*, thereby completing his theological training, Bonhoeffer, at twenty-three, was still two years away from ordination, so he reluctantly left for the United States and a postgraduate fellowship at Union Theological Seminary in New York City. There he formed lasting friendships with Swiss student Erwin Sutz, with whom he shared an appreciation of Barth's theology, and French student Jean Lasserre, who introduced Bonhoeffer to Christian pacifism and influenced his later masterpiece, *The Cost of Discipleship*.

The most significant impact on Bonhoeffer in New York, however, came from his experience of the black Church in Harlem. There he found a gospel message that had substance and was proclaimed from the pulpit "with rapturous passion and vision." There he also got a foretaste of the kind of virulent and systemic prejudice that he would later see back in Germany. But it was the remarkable courage and faith of the black community in response to the hatred they faced that caught Bonhoeffer's attention. Their interaction with him was, he wrote home, "one of the most pleasant and significant events"[3] of his American visit, and their example left an indelible mark on him. He would often speak of "cheap grace" versus "costly grace," the former being a desire to have grace without suffering, resurrection without the cross. For Jesus, grace meant accepting and enduring the cross. It cost God's Son his life. Therefore, Bonhoeffer said, "nothing can be cheap to us which is costly to God."[4] The American black Church understood this, he realized. They knew that the gospel, that grace, "costs people their lives."[5] Bonhoeffer's lament was that so many other Christians did not seem to know or accept this. They continued to want grace at a cheap price.

Bonhoeffer learned something else in this period of his life: the importance of churches working together. In 1931, as he was making his way back to Germany, Bonhoeffer was invited by his pacifist friend Jean Lasserre to attend a conference in Cambridge sponsored by the then relatively new World Alliance of Churches. Through Lasserre and his own research, Bonhoeffer was becoming more convinced that Christians were called to be peacemakers and that they could do this more effectively by breaking out of a provincial mindset and working together. He entered the budding world of the ecumenical movement with high hopes and great enthusiasm for what was possible. It was this combination of a deepening pacifism and a commitment to work across denominational and national lines that made Bonhoeffer particularly attuned to the dangers of Nazism when he returned to Berlin to teach.

By this time, Hitler had gained considerable power, and many students at the seminary were avid followers of this national hero. After all, he had promised a return to greatness for the country and at the same time assured the people that he would not interfere in the Church's affairs. He promoted family values, reined in the youth of the nation and gave them purpose, and helped citizens feel proud once more to be German. The fact that there was an increasingly anti-Jewish component to the Nazi program seemed to go unnoticed by many until years later, when it was too late and Hitler was firmly in control of the nation. But Bonhoeffer's antennae seemed to go up immediately upon his return, which made him something of an anomaly and an outsider at the seminary. But his brief foray into the ecumenical world had given him a larger vision, and there were several students who caught that vision and gathered with him.

A Voice in the Wilderness

It didn't take long for Bonhoeffer to voice his concerns in public, and even less time for the government to react to his criticisms. The first occasion was a radio broadcast given in early 1933, two days after Hitler had been appointed chancellor. Bonhoeffer's address, "The Younger Generation's Altered View of the Concept of Führer," boldly indicted leaders who "set themselves up as gods." Without warning, his microphone was turned off, and Bonhoeffer had his first taste of the kind of censorship that would permeate German life throughout the coming decade. Within weeks, various edicts went forth overthrowing basic civil liberties, including the right to freely assemble, the right of free speech, and freedom from unlawful arrest and detention. Soon Hitler's government had secured the right to enact laws without consulting the legislature. And with the Aryan Clause, those with Jewish blood were banned from civil service jobs. Bonhoeffer's own dear friend Franz Hildebrandt could not serve as a Christian pastor because his mother was Jewish. Within months, Germany had become a fascist state. Bonhoeffer's fears were being realized.

Bonhoeffer seemed to be one of the only ones willing to acknowledge what was happening. The majority of Church members, far from critiquing the new regime, were wholeheartedly embracing it. The so-called German Christians banded together and celebrated what they saw as the divine hand behind Hitler, describing the leader's rise to power as a miracle from God. They defined their brand of faith as "positive Christianity"[6] and focused far less on the scriptures and far more on what they understood as God's working through the Aryan race. Far from challenging Nazi anti-Jewish sentiments, the German Christians actually promulgated this position and very soon began infecting the state Church with their beliefs. Not everyone in the Church agreed with this movement, but unfortunately, not many were willing to stand up and speak out. The Roman Catholic Church also failed to speak out and indeed signed a concordat with Hitler saying that the Nazi leader would not interfere in Catholic Church affairs and that Church leaders would not speak out against the government. Bonhoeffer was virtually alone.

There were some who shared Bonhoeffer's concerns. They called themselves the "Young Reformers," and they quietly spoke out on behalf of Christians of Jewish origin. They were hardly at the same place at which Bonhoeffer found himself, but at least they were not neutral or, worse, complicit with the Nazi policies. Bonhoeffer, for his part, had a more strategic plan of action that he wanted to share with his fellow Christians. He laid out his vision in a theological journal in an April 1933 article titled "The Church and the Jewish Question."[7] Bonhoeffer outlined three possible steps that the Church could take in the face of what it considered inappropriate government actions. First, the Church could directly challenge the state, demanding that it justify its actions—in other words, the Church would act as the conscience of the nation. Second, the Church could recognize its own responsibility to offer aid to victims of illegitimate actions of the state, even if the victims "do not belong to the Christian community." Third, and most provocatively, Bonhoeffer said that the Church was called "not just to bandage the victims under the wheel, but to jam a spoke in the wheel itself." All this he wrote in the specific context of the anti-Jewish actions being taken with impunity by the Nazi government. It was a three-step plan that, intentionally or otherwise, Bonhoeffer himself would carry out.

In the years that followed, events escalated dramatically. A former munitions factory in the outskirts of Dachau became the first concentration camp for the Nazis, and many more were added soon thereafter. The so-called Emergency Measures continued to be issued from Hitler's government, taking away one freedom after another and eventually focusing on those parts of the Church that showed any sign of resistance to Hitler's programs. The young people of the nation were targeted to join the Hitler Youth, where they experienced a complete conditioning program that made them ultimately loyal to Hitler alone. And in November of 1938, just five years after Bonhoeffer issued his warning about where the anti-Jewish propaganda was leading, the hostility against the Jews reached a crescendo on *Kristallnacht*, the Night of Broken Glass, as a wave of destruction swept throughout the land, focused completely on Jewish shops and synagogues. Through these years, Bonhoeffer pushed his fellow Christians to stand and be counted. "The question really is," he said, "Germanism or Christianity."[8]

COMPASSION AND ACTION

There were opportunities for Bonhoeffer to step out of the struggle, if only for a brief respite. In 1934, he traveled to England and there struck up a friendship with Bishop George Bell, who would become a close friend and a strong advocate abroad. Bonhoeffer also considered accepting an invitation to visit Gandhi in India and learn from him about nonviolent resistance, but messages from Germany made it clear that he was desperately needed at home. He returned to serve as teacher and trainer for a secret seminary set up by what was now called the "Confessing Church." The earlier Young Reformers had given way to the Pastors' Emergency League, formed by Bonhoeffer and three other pastors. One of these was Martin Niemöller, who would become such a thorn in Hitler's side that eventually his house was bombed and he was arrested and detained by the Gestapo for eight years as "a personal prisoner of the Führer."⁹ The Pastors' Emergency League in turn led to the creation of the Barmen Declaration, a masterful proclamation of faith written in large part by theologian Karl Barth, and the Confessing Church that was born from it. Finally, here was a group that was prepared to take a stand. Bonhoeffer trained the next generation of ordained leaders in the small coastal town of Finkenwalde, modeling there what Christian community is called to be and reminding members in the midst of the increasing persecution that "suffering is the badge of true discipleship."¹⁰ And yet when the *Kristallnacht* occurred, Bonhoeffer again found himself frustrated by the deafening silence of the faithful.

It was time to do something more. Various secret anti-Nazi opposition groups had arisen; one existed under Hitler's nose in the Abwehr, the Nazi counterintelligence office. Hans von Dohnanyi, Bonhoeffer's brother-in-law, worked as a lawyer for the Abwehr and both shared information with and sought counsel from Dietrich about a conspiracy to overthrow Hitler and set up a new government with the backing of military leaders within and other nations outside. Other members of the Bonhoeffer family were involved in the conspiracy. With war appearing imminent, Bonhoeffer visited England and America once more, only to return to Germany fully committed to do whatever was necessary. He was brought into the Abwehr and became a double agent.

He did not take this step lightly. The war he had dreaded had come. And even as Hitler's troops invaded Poland, the dictator's sterilization program began, initially aimed at those who were developmentally challenged and those who suffered from severe mental illness or epilepsy—the "incurables" as Hitler put it—and eventually targeting the Jews and other "inferior races." For a person of conscience, events had reached an intolerable point. "Mere waiting and looking on," Bonhoeffer asserted later in a 1942 letter, "is not Christian behavior." Those who would follow Jesus, he continued, "are called to compassion and action."¹¹ For Bonhoeffer himself, this meant political involvement. Sadly, his decision to become a double agent working against Hitler was not understood by his fellow leaders in the Confessing Church. To them, Bonhoeffer had defected from their cause and sold out to Hitler by working in his counterintelligence office. It is ironic that the same Christians whom Bonhoeffer had been unable to rouse to action in earlier years now doubted his true loyalties as he embarked on his most sacrificial work.

Bonhoeffer didn't waver in his work in these war years. While reporting on the ecumenical movement to the Abwehr, he simultaneously used the time traveling abroad to try to convince various Church leaders of the need to support the German resistance against Hitler. It was a dangerous game he was playing, with the stakes incredibly high. At the same time, he continued to write, focusing his energies on a project he had long desired to be his magnum opus, *Ethics.* In this book, he pondered the questions with which he was involved on a practical level. The farther he moved forward, the more convinced was Bonhoeffer that a life of faith demanded involvement in the struggles of the day or, as he put it, "living completely in the world."[12] Writing to his dear friend and eventual biographer, Eberhard Bethge, he explained this:

> I mean living unreservedly in life duties, problems, successes and failures, experiences and perplexities. In so doing we throw ourselves completely into the arms of God, taking seriously not our own sufferings, but those of God in the world."[13]

In the end, it wasn't his involvement in the large-scale conspiracy to overthrow Hitler that led to Bonhoeffer's arrest, but a small plan that helped fourteen Jews escape from Germany. When his brother-in-law Hans was arrested in 1943 and his house searched, the trail led directly to Dietrich Bonhoeffer.

THE END, THE BEGINNING

After his initial days of despair behind bars, even contemplating suicide "because basically I am already dead,"[14] Bonhoeffer began to adapt to prison life. His fellow prisoners, and even many of the guards, respected and appreciated what they saw in him. His family stayed in as close contact as possible, writing often. As they had prepared long before, knowing full well the possibility of detention that now had come, they had developed a clever code to send important information back and forth without discovery. Bonhoeffer's imprisonment was perhaps hardest on his fiancée. Although he had long warned his "underground" students against marriage because of the obvious dangers of arrest, Dietrich himself had fallen in love with Maria von Wedemeyer, granddaughter of a resistance supporter. Now, Maria could content herself only with letters and brief visits, until even that was impossible. Bonhoeffer's worries were far more for Maria and his family than for himself.

During his time in prison, the conspirators made one last assassination attempt against Hitler, which would become famous as "Project Valkyrie" (and eventually would even become the subject of a 2002 Hollywood movie starring Tom Cruise, though no mention is made in it of Bonhoeffer). Colonel Claus Schenk von Stauffenberg carried an explosive device into a meeting at Hitler's Wolfschanze retreat. The bomb went off, and four members of Hitler's staff were killed and the rest injured, but Hitler himself survived. Even as he began to speak of himself as invulnerable, Hitler ordered the execution of those involved in the plot. It would take some time before Bonhoeffer's name would be linked to the conspiracy, but he and the others knew it was only a matter of time. A final escape effort was planned for him, involving both family and a sympathetic guard, but Dietrich refused to go along when he learned that his brother Klaus had also just been imprisoned. Bonhoeffer would stay and wait for release from prison following an Allied victory—or release into the larger life. In a letter to Maria only months before his execution, he wrote a poem that spoke of "the forces of good" that would "firm up our courage for what comes our way."[15] Courage and faith were his close companions.

The Allies did come to Berlin and victory was indeed theirs. But victory came too late for Bonhoeffer and his fellow prisoners. On April 9, 1945, Dietrich Bonhoeffer was led to the gallows where he would take his last breath, but not before saying to a fellow prisoner who survived and passed along these words: "This is the end—for me the beginning of life."[16] In the years that followed, Bonhoeffer's many writings would find their way into the hands of Christians everywhere, and the extent of his sacrifice would become evident. Confessing Church members who had at one point wondered whether their friend had betrayed all that he once taught now wondered how they ever could have doubted him. And as more private correspondences to his family and his fiancée have become public in more recent years, the depth of his feelings, his passion, his hopes and dreams have become evident as well.

DEALING WITH DANGER

With courage and faith, Deitrich Bonhoeffer worked tirelessly against the Nazi regime and heroically put the gospel into action during a horrendous period in history. For speaking out truth to power, he was revealed to be a threat to the secular powers and even to some in the Church who tried to placate those powers. In this way, he followed in the footsteps of Jesus, who had stood up to both the Roman overlords who saw him as an insurrectionist and the religious leaders who labeled him a blasphemer. Like Jesus, Bonhoeffer stood his ground, unbowed by the powers against him. And like Jesus, he was treated as an enemy of the state and executed.

Heroes are often put on a pedestal, either to revere or pull down. But Bonhoeffer was proof that heroes truly are ordinary people who see what is needed—what everyone else should see, but all too often do not—and then do the right thing. Bonhoeffer did not seek imprisonment and death. He was no masochist. But he was a martyr, and a willing one at that. Toward the end, he wrote a poem titled "Who Am I?" in which he recognized the disconnect between what people often believed him to be and what he as a very real human being actually was: "They often tell me I would step from my prison cell poised, cheerful, and sturdy, like a nobleman from his country estate." But he knew at heart that he was "restless, yearning, sick, like a bird in a cage."[17]

What made Dietrich Bonhoeffer remarkable was that even as he acknowledged his own failings and fears in that poem, he also affirmed, "Whoever I am, you know me, O God. You know I am yours."[18] This was his real secret, the piece of knowledge that kept him going when all seemed to fall in around him. And it was this knowledge that allowed him to die as he had lived, willingly—if not easily—enduring the cost of discipleship.

For Reflection

1. From the earliest days of the Nazi rise to power, Bonhoeffer was one of very few who called the Church to beware. What if he had been wrong? How do we know when we need to speak out and when to stay silent?

2. For Bonhoeffer, the formation of Christian leaders was crucial to the work of the gospel. What are some ways that you can help in the formation of faithful Christian leaders today?

3. Bonhoeffer felt dread and even self-doubt while in prison, yet pressed on in faith nonetheless. When you have found yourself near despair? What has kept you going?

For Further Reading

Bethge, Eberhard. *Dietrich Bonhoeffer: A Biography*. Revised and edited by Victoria J. Barnett. Minneapolis: Fortress, 2000.

Bonhoeffer, Dietrich. *Letters and Papers from Prison: An Abridged Edition*. Norwich, UK: SCM Press, 2001.

———. *No Rusty Swords: Letters, Lectures, and Notes 1928–1936*. New York: Harper & Row, 1965.

Raum, Elizabeth. *Dietrich Bonhoeffer: Called by God*. New York: Continuum, 2003.

Schlingensiepen, Ferdinand. *Dietrich Bonhoeffer: 1906–1945*. New York: T & T Clark, 2010.

For an inspiring documentary of the pastor and martyr, see *Bonhoeffer*. DVD. Directed by Martin Doblmeier and featuring the voice of Klaus Maria Brandauer. New York: First Run Features, 2004.

10

JANANI LUWUM

The Revivalist

While the opportunity is there, I preach the gospel with all my might, and my conscience is clear before God.

—JANANI LUWUM, 1976

When pilgrims and tourists visit London's Westminster Abbey, one of the first sights awaiting them is a collection of ten stone sculptures of twentieth-century martyrs in what used to be empty niches. There, standing beside figures like Martin Luther King Jr. and Maximilian Kolbe, is Janani Luwum, the late archbishop of Uganda. It is impossible for outsiders looking in at a country controlled by a tyrant to understand the depth of the pain experienced by those living within such a system. It is equally impossible to comprehend the remarkable sacrifice of those who stand up to such a tyrant. At the time of his conversion to Christ, a young Luwum proudly declared, "I am ready to die in the army of Jesus."[1] Years later, that is exactly what he did, standing up to a despot and sacrificing himself in the process. In his life and through his death, Luwum became one of the most beloved and influential leaders of the modern Church in Africa.

FROM *BALOKOLE* TO BISHOP

Born in 1922 in a part of Uganda close to the border of Sudan, the tall, powerful Luwum was a leader from his earliest days. Among his Acholi tribe, he stood out. People sought him out, respected him, deferred to him. Naturally, without any hint of pretention, he excelled in academics, art, and a host of other fields. So it was little surprise that his parents imagined for his future the role of tribal chief. His path, however, took a different turn. It was after he had graduated Boroboro Teacher Training College and was working as a teacher that Janani Luwum, a Christian by birth and lineage, now became one by personal experience and choice. In January 1948, listening to the words of a *balokole* preacher, Janani encountered Jesus for himself and was converted to a deeper life in Christ. The *balokole* was a charismatic revival movement that arose in the 1930s throughout East Africa, in Uganda, Kenya, Tanzania, Rwanda, and Burundi. It was viewed with some suspicion by established churches, whose members were prime targets for the *balokole* evangelistic efforts. With a focus on the immediacy of the Holy Spirit's work in individual lives, *balokole* preachers shared a message of radical repentance, challenging those they saw as nominal Christians to confess their sins and, through the power of Christ's death on the cross, to "walk in the light."

Not all was bright and cheery with the movement, though. It had its own internal struggles and in later years split into disagreeing factions, which themselves then split again. But in those earlier days, wherever the *balokole* went, dramatic conversions occurred. People professed their faith in Jesus, gave up habits such as drinking, and often displayed visible signs such as speaking in ecstatic tongues. And on that January day in 1948, with tears streaming down his face, Janani Luwum joined the *balokole* list of converts.

Many years later, Luwum recalled the power of that moment: "When I was converted, after realizing that my sins were forgiven and the implications of Jesus's death and resurrection, I was overwhelmed by a sense of joy and peace. I suddenly found myself climbing a tree to tell those in the school compound to repent and turn to Jesus Christ. The reality of Jesus overwhelmed me, and it still does."[2]

Conversions are often described as mountaintop experiences, and the true test for new believers occurs when they come down from the mountain to the very real struggles that await in what the psalmist called "the valley of the shadow of death" (Psalm 23:4). For Luwum, those struggles came hard and fast. Not even a month had passed following his conversion before he and other *balokole* were arrested for "disturbing the peace" with their message of repentance and temperance. But Luwum was undeterred: "The wooden bars at the window of this tiny cell cannot separate us from the love of God, nor stop us from proclaiming the message of salvation."[3] The great difficulty facing Luwum was not opposition from those outside the Church but suspicion from those within who remained unsure of the loyalty of the *balokole* movement's members. The *balokole* leaders noticed this skepticism and took steps to earn trust by having Luwum, an educated *balokole*, seek full-time ordained ministry in the Church of Uganda. An obedient Luwum left his vocation as a teacher and became first a deacon and then a priest in the Church.

Ordained an Anglican priest in 1956, Luwum's leadership qualities again caught the attention of the powers that be. In this case, two bishops of northern Uganda were impressed enough to send him to St. Augustine's College in Canterbury, England, the traditional training place for future leaders in the worldwide Anglican Communion. It wasn't just the bishops who believed in Luwum. A lot of people back home were eagerly awaiting Luwum's return, convinced that he would be some kind of über-pastor.

Instead, to the surprise of everyone, especially Luwum, his return to Uganda and pastoral duties in Lira Palwo proved to be disappointing. Instead of growth, he only witnessed decline and apathy among the Church's membership. No matter what he tried, nothing seemed to work.

Of course, his story did not end there. Pulled out of the no-win situation, Luwum was placed at Buwalasi Theological College, where he excelled. Only ten years after his ordination, Luwum was made provincial secretary of the Church of Uganda, a highly influential position in which he again did well. When all the bishops of the Anglican Communion met in 1968 for the Lambeth Conference, the once-a-decade worldwide Church meeting, he was present as a consultant. It was only a matter of time before he was made a bishop.

In 1969 the new Diocese of Northern Uganda was created, and Luwum was named its first bishop. He was also the first of his tribe to become a bishop, although this was less remarkable than the trust he had earned in spite of his background as one of the *balokole*, who were still viewed by many mainstream Ugandan Christians with some suspicion. Luwum came into his new vocation with energy and a focus on financial stewardship and care for his clergy. "Take the hoe out of your pastor's hand" was Luwum's way of admonishing Church members to make sure that their clergy were doing the ministry to which they were called, and from which all would benefit, instead of having to worry about their livelihood and sustenance. Outreach to those in need, especially lepers, was also a priority for the new bishop. Most of all, Luwum had a passion for making the good news available to all who would hear. Less than a year after taking office, he initiated a massive preaching crusade with over a hundred evangelists and missioners preaching and leading revival meetings. His theme was simple and scriptural: to call the people from darkness to light.

DARKNESS DESCENDING

Christianity in Uganda had known dark times from its inception. The Martyrs of Uganda, whose feast day is still commemorated by the Church, were companions in the 1880s who were burned at the stake for their faith, much like Thomas Cranmer and his fellow English reformers three centuries before. The only "crime" committed by those early Ugandan martyrs was to proclaim Jesus as Lord, a claim that was seen as politically threatening by Mwanga, ruler of the land at that time. Since then, Uganda had become a protectorate of the British Empire. Then, in Luwum's own time, Uganda became an independent nation, and former prime minister–turned–president Milton Obote showed an apparent respect for the Church and its leaders, even appearing at Luwum's own consecration service as bishop in 1969. But in 1971, only five years after Obote took control of the Ugandan government from the mostly ceremonial president, changed the constitution, and made a complete break from Britain, a military coup d'état occurred. The leader of the coup was the very person who had helped Obote achieve his position: Idi Amin Dada.

The son of a Roman Catholic convert to Islam, Amin received only the equivalent of a fourth-grade education before leaving school and eventually joining the British colonial army as an assistant cook. Though he was considered to be largely illiterate by many, Amin was a physically powerful—and emotionally commanding—man. He quickly rose in rank until achieving the post of commander of the armed forces. It is interesting to see how Amin and Obote, formerly collaborators and co-conspirators against President Mutesa, now turned on each other, with Obote afraid of Amin's military power and preparing to arrest the general for misappropriation of funds. Amin's coup took place, however, before any such arrest could be made. At first, Amin promised the people that he had no interest in politics and would help prepare the country for democratic elections—a promise that lasted exactly one week. He went on to call himself "His Excellency, President for Life," and later "Conqueror of the British Empire." Others would instead refer to him simply as "the Butcher of Uganda." Estimates of those killed during his reign range anywhere from eighty thousand to as many as half a million people.

Like so many, Bishop Luwum watched helplessly as Amin began his persecution of entire ethnic groups, first focusing on Luwum's own Acholi tribe, as well as the nearby Lango tribe. Massacres resulted, along with an increasing number of disappearances. For many, a sense of dread hung over the land. For his part, Luwum tried to gather support from his fellow bishops. When they together finally secured a meeting with Amin, the general's explanation was simple: "The enemy has to be rooted out." Purges continued, and critics of the government, including even a chief justice, were murdered. The Asians were also targeted, not for execution but rather for expulsion; some eighty thousand Pakistanis and Indians, many of whom were second-generation residents carrying British passports, were ousted from Uganda. The free world protested to no avail. Uganda's ties with Britain were cut, and new partnerships were made with the despotic state of Libya under Muammar Gaddafi, as well as with the Soviet Union, which supplied Amin with the weapons he required. Unsurprisingly, Israelis living within Uganda were expelled, too, which strengthened Amin's relationship with Gaddafi and with the ruler of Saudi Arabia. The United States ambassador called for a break in diplomatic ties with Amin's government, describing it as "racist, erratic and unpredictable, brutal, inept, bellicose, irrational, ridiculous, and militaristic."[4] Amin himself was depicted by many foreign newspapers and publications as a buffoon, but the much more disturbing image of what he was doing was offered by a former Ugandan official–turned–defector, whose exposé of Amin's regime was appropriately titled *A State of Blood*. For many, darkness truly had descended upon the land.

It was in 1974, in the midst of this uneasy political context, that Janani Luwum, *balokole* and bishop, was elected as archbishop of the entire Anglican Church of Uganda, succeeding his friend and mentor, Archbishop Sabiti. Luwum immediately stressed that the Church's job is always to help people move their faith in Jesus from their heads to their hearts. The preacher at his installation went even farther, reminding Luwum and the people with him of the cost that they had to be willing to pay if they were to be serious about following Jesus. But perhaps Luwum could be forgiven for not immediately seeing the cost, as President Amin did the unexpected: he reached out to Luwum, sending for him, confiding in him, seeking his counsel. Throughout his time as archbishop, Luwum faced criticism from some who believed that he was overly comfortable with Amin and the government. Luwum was quick to respond, "Even the president needs friends," and again, "He is also a child of God."[5] Luwum avoided conflict and instead sought out avenues of mediation. "Come let us reason together, says the Lord" (Isaiah 1:18) was one of his favorite scriptural passages. He tried to see the best in everyone, and when that wasn't possible, he tried to free those he saw as prisoners of their own evil. Luwum's boundless energy was matched only by his optimism and ability to forgive, which he saw as necessary for anyone who would follow in the footsteps of Jesus.

It wasn't long before the results of Amin's outlandish actions became visible to everyone. The sudden, massive deportation of Asians had a debilitating effect on the economy, and the increased militarization of the government—with the substantial funding it required—contributed further to the economic downturn that swept the land. There were nonfinancial ramifications of Amin's policy changes as well, especially regarding his government appointments. At one time, he had called together all the bishops and forced them to find ways to reconcile with one another for the sake of unity. "I saved the Church!" he boasted.[6] Any illusions those leaders might have had about his support of the faith flew out the window as they saw Amin get rid of Christian members of the government, replacing them with Muslims. Amin himself came from one of the then-few predominantly Muslim tribal groups. It did not take long before he moved from being simply pro-Muslim to being anti-Christian. Christian missionaries, both Roman Catholic and Anglican, were deported without warning. The gift to Amin of a gold sword from King Faisal of Saudi Arabia came with the note, "With this sword, make your country Muslim." Church leaders grew increasingly nervous: where would this all end? In the midst of the anxiety, Archbishop Luwum served as a beacon of hope and strength. With more and more missionaries gone, he called for more indigenous evangelists to proclaim the good news. "I do not want to be archbishop of a dead Church," he insisted, "but of a live one!"[7]

DAILY, DAILY SING THE PRAISES

From its beginnings in Uganda with the arrival of the first missionaries in 1877, Christianity had grown from the blood of martyrs. As the Church approached its centennial, it seemed as if it would enter its next century the same way. There was greater repression by the government and increasing violence on the streets between Christians and Muslims. Luwum stepped up to promote a nonviolent way forward for all Ugandans. In August 1976, when the military raided a university in Makerere in response to peaceful student protests against the murder of a Jewish girl, Luwum immediately went to the campus to seek protection for the protesting students. And in response to the Christian-Muslim struggles, he took to heart the example of a local region and called on the Roman Catholic cardinal, the Orthodox bishop, and the sheikh mufti of Uganda, the chief Islamic leader, to join him at the Church of Uganda conference center in Lweza, a few miles outside of the capital city of Kampala, to discuss ways they could all work together for the greater good.

Though the Orthodox leader was unable to attend, the cardinal and the sheikh mufti, as well as other representatives from all three religious groups with them, did, and Luwum was asked to chair the meeting, in which they faced head-on the problems, anxieties, and rumors sweeping throughout the country. They spoke of the "jealousy, personal animosity, paying back evil for evil"[8] that lay at the heart of the conflicts. They offered recommendations to and asked for greater communication and cooperation from the government. Amin was, to put it mildly, not pleased. For the first time in memory, the faith communities had taken a stand against the government, and Luwum was seen as the ringleader. His message became more and more pointed; his concern for what was happening all around him more obvious. His cry was simply this: "Uganda is killing Uganda!"[9] This was not the kind of language that Amin wanted to hear. The general issued statements critical of Church leaders, suggesting that they were becoming troublemakers, disruptive to the civil peace that Amin supposedly offered the people. And still there were those who believed that Luwum had not said enough, not done enough, to challenge the government. He was embattled on two fronts.

In December 1976, Luwum preached on the radio a sermon critical of the government, resulting in the broadcast being taken off the air. Despite the concern of some that he was not being critical enough, there was no doubt in Amin's mind that the archbishop was more than a nuisance; he was now a threat. Two months later, Luwum's home was raided by security forces. Shocked and dismayed, the archbishop and many of Uganda's bishops wrote an open letter of protest, now sharply pointing a finger at the military-run government and its abuse of power: "The gun that was meant to protect … the Ugandan citizen and his property is increasingly being used against the Ugandan to take away his life and his property," wrote Luwum in a 1977 letter to Amin. For his part, Amin would not let this pass. Only a few days later, both Janani and Mary Luwum, his wife, were interrogated by the tyrant in the presidential palace, with questions thrown at them about their involvement in a "conspiracy" against Amin. Having denied any such conspiracy, they were allowed to go home, with a stern warning that Luwum should concentrate on his religious duties and stay clear of any political statements. However, two days after this, on February 16, 1977, Luwum and other bishops were brought to a large rally in Kampala, where "confessions" of alleged co-conspirators were read, marking Luwum as a key figure in an attempt to smuggle arms into the country and lead a coup against Amin. Luwum denied the trumped-up charges, but before the day had ended he was arrested.

Paraded before soldiers and others loyal to Amin, the accusations were again made against Luwum and his companions. When asked what should be done with them, the cries of the onlookers went up, "Kill them!" For Luwum, it must have seemed all too familiar, remembering that these very words were spoken at the trial of Jesus himself. He must have known what fate awaited him. As he was separated from colleagues and led away, his words were brief: "I see God's hand in this."[10] The details of what happened after that are known only to God and those who were actually present. The government's official story is that, while en route by car to an interrogation center with two other prisoners, one or more of them tried to overtake the driver, resulting in a crash. But it was said soon thereafter that when Luwum's body was seen, it was riddled with bullet wounds, shot multiple times at close range. The body was buried secretly, and no autopsy was performed.

Unsurprisingly, the government refused requests for a public memorial service. After all, this man was considered by Amin to have been a traitor. Despite this, thousands gathered at the cathedral in Kampala at the grave that had been set aside next to that of

Bishop Hannington, the missionary bishop who had been mar-
tyred in the earliest years of Christianity in Uganda. Now, on the
eve of the Church's centennial celebrations, Archbishop Luwum
was proclaimed the first martyr of the Church of Uganda's second
century. The people broke out spontaneously in the words of the
famous hymn sung by Hannington and those first martyrs, a
hymn alleged to have been on Luwum's and his companions' lips
as they were led to their own execution: "Daily, daily sing the
praises of the city God has made...."

Idi Amin, like Pontius Pilate before him, ended his reign not
in glory but in disgrace. Luwum's widow, Mary, and their children
were held under virtual house arrest but eventually escaped and
made their way safely to Kenya. As for the Church, instead of
dying out under Amin's persecutions, its membership gained
strength and increased in numbers. Like the words of the prayer
used to commemorate Luwum's life and witness to Jesus,
Christians in Uganda, and indeed throughout all of Africa, took to
heart the archbishop's noble example, demonstrating "boldness to
confess the Name of our Savior Jesus Christ before the rulers of
this world, and courage to die for this faith."[11]

DEALING WITH DANGER

Like other martyrs before him, Janani Luwum stood up to a dictator and challenged his authority. Although he was quick to admit
that Amin was a child of God, he did not forget that he himself
was a child of God as well, and so were all the people of his beloved
Uganda. This was the great equalizer, this view of all people
through the eyes of the Creator. The generosity in spirit that this
view engendered in Luwum is what enabled him to pray for Amin
and even continue attending government functions when others
stood by in wonder, and it is also what enabled Luwum to stand
firm against Amin when he saw no such generosity of spirit on the
part of the tyrant toward the people. Luwum had a pastor's heart,

and as chief priest and pastor of the people of Uganda, he understood the importance of standing with them and standing up for them when needed. Grounded in the teachings of his past in the *balokole* revival movement, as well as his own readings of leaders like Martin Luther King Jr., Luwum gladly pursued a nonviolent course of resistance against Amin. His faith and faithfulness infuriated the dictator, but Luwum knew that someone greater than Amin was standing by his side.

For Reflection

1. Janani Luwum faced criticism from both sides for his approach to Church-state relations. In our more democratic context, what does it mean to stand for Christ and for God's children in need?

2. Regarding Idi Amin, Luwum said that "even the president needs friends." What does it mean to show "friendship" to leaders when they are acting clearly in the wrong?

3. It is not difficult to see how Luwum was influenced by figures such as Gandhi and Martin Luther King Jr. Who are persons you have not met but whose life and teachings have influenced you?

For Further Reading

Bergman, Susan, ed. *Martyrs: Contemporary Writers on Modern Lives of Faith*. Maryknoll, NY: Orbis Books, 1998.

Ford, Margaret. *Janani: The Making of a Martyr*. New York: Harper & Row, 1978.

Hefley, James C., and Marti Hefley. *By Their Blood: Christian Martyrs of the Twentieth Century*. 2nd ed. Grand Rapids: Baker Book House, 1996.

11

OSCAR ROMERO

The Advocate

I have no ambition for power, and so with complete freedom I tell the powerful what is good and what is bad.

—OSCAR ROMERO, MARCH 23, 1980

Archbishop Oscar Romero, at the end of his ministry working for the people of El Salvador, insisted that his faith compelled him to speak out boldly against the political forces that sought to silence him. Less than twenty-four hours later, he lay dead in a chapel, gunned down at the altar during Mass.

It was unthinkable that such a horrific thing could happen. Just three years earlier, it would have been equally unthinkable that such a thing would happen to a quiet bookworm like Romero. "Hero" and "martyr" weren't words that anyone had associated with him before his appointment to the highest ecclesiastical office in his land. It was almost inconceivable that he could ever pose a threat to the establishment great enough that some would order his assassination. And yet, as with Jesus, in whose name he served so faithfully, those last three years of Romero's life proved to be crucial ones. Few Church leaders have had so powerful an impact in such a brief time. Few have left such an extensive, global legacy. Yet this was a cleric who was chosen for his position precisely because it was thought he would not make waves.

THE SAFE CHOICE

He was born Óscar Arnulfo Romero y Goldámez in 1917 in Ciudad Barrios, El Salvador. Hired out by his father as an apprentice to a carpenter at thirteen, Romero instead felt drawn to the ordained life. Completing his theological studies in Rome, he was ordained to the priesthood when he was twenty-five. A pastor's heart combined with a scholar's mind in Romero, and he spent the majority of his ministry as a parish priest and a diocesan secretary, while always cherishing his books and the truths he learned from them. Romero was a conservative in Church matters, a traditionalist who struggled with some of the changes in the Church brought about by the Second Vatican Council—a meeting convened by Pope John XXIII in 1962 to open the door and "let some fresh air in." He was even more skeptical of decisions reached at Medellín.

Toward the end of the 1960s, a group of Latin American bishops met at Medellín, Colombia, to discuss Vatican II's pronouncements and how they could be implemented in their own context. What came out of this conference of bishops was nothing short of revolutionary. At the opening of their statement on "Poverty of the Church," published on September 6, 1968, the gathered leaders abandoned a long-standing course of supporting the societal status quo, "remain[ing] indifferent in the face of the tremendous social injustices existent in Latin America," and instead committed themselves to taking seriously the "deafening cry" for liberation that came from "the throats of millions."[1] In a remarkable piece of transparency, the bishops acknowledged the popular perception that "the hierarchy, the clergy, the religious are rich and allied with the rich."[2] That had to change. It was time, the bishops declared, to be counted with the poor and the repressed. It was a remarkable document, and Oscar Romero did not approve of it.

It was not that Romero spoke out against the Medellín conference; that was not his way. But as a traditionalist who did not believe that the Church should involve itself with what appeared to be political issues, he was not pleased. Meanwhile, he moved up in the Church's hierarchy, first becoming auxiliary bishop of San Salvador in 1970 and then, four years later, bishop of Santiago de María, the rural diocese in which he had grown up. Romero worked hard and kept a low profile, even as the situation in El Salvador deteriorated, the government grew more corrupt, the divide between the wealthy minority and the destitute majority increased, and more priests found themselves drawn into what was being called "liberation theology," a movement especially strong in Latin America that sees the teachings of Jesus as a call for liberation from unjust economic, political, and social conditions. As with the participants of the Medellín conference, a growing number of younger clergy spoke of God's "preferential treatment of the poor" and involved themselves directly in the people's struggle. The elderly Salvadoran archbishop, Luis Chávez y González, sympathized with these priests and even encouraged them until, after decades in leadership, he retired. Surprisingly to many, the Vatican named Romero to succeed Chávez. Some colleagues noted that he was a safe choice, a conservative who would not rock the boat, a placeholder to keep things steady until a clear long-term decision could be reached. Romero himself later spoke of himself as "frail," and many apparently believed it. They were wrong.

A TRUE PASTOR

Though many were shocked with Romero's boldness after becoming archbishop, perhaps they shouldn't have been. After all, despite his conflict-averse tendencies, Romero had always had the heart of a true pastor. As a bishop in his rural homeland, he saw firsthand the struggles of the landless poor. He would see far worse after becoming archbishop, but his earlier experience stirred his conscience and raised questions within him. The way was prepared for a catalyst moment that would transform Romero. That moment was the murder of his dear friend Father Rutilio Grande.

Grande had been a classmate of Romero's at seminary. In 1965, he was appointed director of social action projects at the seminary in San Salvador, and he also served as professor of pastoral theology. The combination was ideal for Grande, who remained a friend to Romero and even served as master of ceremonies at the latter's installation as bishop in Santiago de María. A strong proponent for the poor and dispossessed, Grande understood and shared in their pain and helped establish Christian Base Communities, or cell churches, which were viewed by local landowners as a threat to their power. Government officials also were threatened by Grande, who spoke out against the abuses he saw. Grande proclaimed:

> I am fully aware that very soon the Bible and the Gospels will not be allowed to cross the border. All that will reach us will be the covers, since all the pages are subversive, it is said. If Jesus crosses the border at Chalatenango, they will not allow him to enter. They would accuse him … of being an agitator.[3]

These provocative words led to his murder on March 12, 1977, as Grande, an older parishioner, and a young boy were brutally slaughtered by machine-gun fire while returning from a baptism service in a neighboring region.

The murder of a priest was unheard of. The people of El Salvador were stunned, and none more so than the new archbishop. Seeing the bodies and hearing from peasants story after story of repression and nighttime disappearances, Romero demanded a government investigation into the murder—which, unsurprisingly, never came. On March 14, 1977, in response to fabricated accounts about Grande in national newspapers, Romero issued a bulletin insisting that the true reason for Grande's death was "his prophetic and pastoral efforts to raise the consciousness of the people ... making them aware of their dignity as individuals." Romero, who previously had been icy toward the reforms of Vatican II, began to change his view, continuing in that same March 14 statement: "This post–Vatican Council ecclesiastical effort is certainly not agreeable to everyone. It disturbs many, and to end it, it was deemed necessary to terminate its proponent, Father Rutilio Grande."

Grande's murder awakened something in Romero. The very next Sunday, as a protest to the killings, he cancelled Masses throughout the archdiocese and held a single Mass in the cathedral at San Salvador. There, Romero himself addressed the crowds, calling for an end to the violence, a message he would proclaim again and again in the following three years.

It's hard not to think of the Hebrew Bible story of the Hebrew prophets Elijah and Elisha: When Elijah was taken up to heaven, he left behind his mantle and a "double portion" of his spirit for Elisha, who went on to an even bolder, more far-reaching prophetic ministry than his predecessor's (2 Kings 2:1–9). In much the same way, Grande's pastoral and prophetic spirit seemed to fill Romero, who took on the task of speaking truth to power and became a voice for the voiceless. Not long after Grande's death, the government closed down the late pastor's parish church, converting it into barracks for soldiers and desecrating the bread and wine of Holy Communion. Romero was aghast—and ready to respond. The formerly nonconfrontational cleric went head to head against the military presence, and he and the people ultimately prevailed. At the church's reopening, Romero preached a powerful message:

> You should know that you have not suffered alone, for you
> are the Church. You are the people of God. You are Jesus in
> the here and now. He is crucified in you just as surely as he
> was crucified two thousand years ago. And you should
> know that your pain and your suffering, like his, will con-
> tribute to El Salvador's redemption.[4]

While it's easy to hear Grande's influence in such words, the
nuances were pure Romero. He did not simply repeat the by-this-
time expected calls for justice for the people. Romero went far
deeper theologically, seeing Jesus's own crucifixion replayed in the
suffering of the people. With a few words he transformed them
from victims of an unjust regime into co-redeemers with Jesus for
the entire country.

Romero recognized that liberation had to mean more than
simply escaping oppression. While some clergy were taking up
arms alongside their people to fight the enemy, Romero saw this as
no more effective in the long run than when the apostle Peter drew
a sword and cut off a soldier's ear when Jesus was arrested the night
before his crucifixion (Luke 22:50). On November 27, 1977, only
a few months after Father Grande had been killed and the parish
church in Aguilares desecrated and then reclaimed, Romero
reminded Salvadoran Christians that their response could not be
"the violence of the sword, the violence of hatred," but must
instead be what he called "the violence of love, of brotherhood, the
violence that wills to beat the weapons into sickles for work."[5] This
was a very different message of hope for those who would listen.
He spoke in strong, even aggressive terms, but about love. This was
the beginning of a uniquely prophetic message worthy of Gandhi
and Martin Luther King Jr.; it showed just how broad and deep
was the pastoral heart of Romero. Until the day he died, the archbishop saw his vocation as being the chief shepherd of all the people, both oppressed and oppressors alike. Again and again, he

reached out to those who crucified Jesus anew in their oppressive, heinous acts and offered them God's pardon and forgiveness:

> I would like to say as a brother to all those friends whose consciences are uneasy because they have sinned against God and neighbor: You cannot be happy that way; the God of love is calling you. He wants to forgive you, he wants to save you.[6]

Romero had been underestimated by virtually everyone before becoming archbishop, and as archbishop he was misunderstood by everyone except the poor and the oppressed, who found in him a leader to trust and follow. They came to him from all across the country, bringing photographs of loved ones who had disappeared in the night. They shared with him stories of fear and frustration. They looked to him as their voice, and through his preaching and his weekly radio broadcasts, he in turn reminded them of their responsibility to stand up for what they knew to be right. Knowing that at any moment the government could close down the radio station he used, Romero called on each believer to become "a microphone, a radio station, a loudspeaker."[7] As their pastor, he was doing more than overseeing or protecting his flock. He was empowering them.

ACCUSATIONS FROM BOTH SIDES

Romero's increasingly bold words and actions did not attract followers only. Opponents arose all around him and, most interestingly, came from both political extremes. In June 1979, he spoke with some bemusement of how the far right accused him of being a Communist at the same time that the far left accused him of joining the right. He seemed to make a lot of people very nervous. The Vatican itself grew more concerned with Romero's growing reputation as someone who sided with the poor. At one point, he even had to defend himself publicly against claims that he was at odds in some way with the pope. Romero's response was clear and heartfelt: "I would rather die a thousand times than be a schismatic bishop!"[8]

Even so, Salvadoran clergy did divide over Romero. Some bishops did not appreciate the rift he was causing between the Church and the government. Until full investigations were conducted into the deaths and disappearances, he refused to participate in official state functions. Despite some hope when a new government came to power, it quickly became evident that the repression of the people would continue. The archbishop remained resolute in his decision to stand apart from the government and speak truth to power—so predictably he was often accused of being a political instigator. He responded that what he did in standing up against injustice was not engaging in politics, but rather fulfilling the prophetic mission that is "the duty of God's people."[9] Both state officials and fellow Church leaders expressed their growing displeasure.

There were priests and freedom fighters, on the other hand, who felt equally frustrated with Romero, for despite his emboldened calls for an end to the oppression, he made it clear that he did not support armed resistance, especially by his clergy. His offers of forgiveness for soldiers who repented of their actions seemed nonsensical to those who could only find feeling in their hearts for the victims. He spoke of Jesus being fully incarnated in those who fight for freedom, but that fight was for Romero a nonviolent one, with the Church sharing in the pain and persecution but not picking up guns. He who once had been critical of the Medellín conference now gladly cited its challenge to Christians to be peacemakers. To priests who chose the way of force, Romero countered with his call for the "force of peace."

Not only did Romero change his mind about Medellín, he also modified his earlier views on the Church's complex relationship with Marxism in Latin America. At the start of his term as archbishop, he was clear in his mind about the absolute distinction between Communism and Christianity. In January 1978, he spoke unequivocally of the Church's "rejection" of Communist "slander" about religion being the people's opium. In December of the same year, he contrasted the Church's solidarity with the poor with some kind of "Marxist dialectic." But by that time he also had begun to see the failings of the Roman Catholic Church in the face of the plight of the poor. It's easy to hear the exasperation in his voice as he lamented, "How shameful to think that perhaps pagans, people with no faith in Christ, may be better than we and nearer to God's reign," and again in the same address, "Outside the limits of Catholicism perhaps is more faith, more holiness."[10]

Romero displayed an understanding heart when it came to those who distanced themselves from what they found to be an uncaring Church. But he was very tough on clergy who took what he believed to be the easy way out by arming themselves and supporting guerilla forces. In April 1979, he went so far as to beg the people's forgiveness on behalf of all bishops and priests for "not having shown all the fortitude the Gospel asks in serving the people we must lead."

More and more, Romero began to challenge any and all institutional structures that perpetuated repression of the people. "It is not God's will," he asserted, "for some to have everything and others to have nothing."[11] Even as he remained adamant that he was not a supporter of socialism, he also was quick to challenge unchecked capitalism. Or more accurately, he was quick to differentiate the Church from either a socialist or capitalist agenda. While others believed that such differentiation meant he should stay out of all political issues, Romero instead saw that the Church—as the voice of the voiceless—was the best instrument for providing a check and balance to both ends of the political spectrum, challenging both when such challenge was needed. As the people's voice, he sent a letter to President Jimmy Carter, entreating him not to send any more arms to El Salvador, as they were being used to kill more people. Involving himself this directly into the situation simply made Romero an even bigger target for opponents' critiques—and potentially for far more deadly attacks.

Rising Up

As early as January 1979, Romero became aware of plots against his life, but he seemed to be unsurprised and undismayed. What a difference from the person he was before Father Grande's death—a quiet bookworm who wanted more than anything to avoid rocking the boat. Now Romero was doing more than just rocking the boat—he was turning it upside down, and he showed no sign of stepping down in the face of threats against him. "I was told this week that I should be careful, that something was being plotted against my life. I trust in the Lord, and I know that the ways of Providence protect one who tries to serve him."[12] As the year progressed, he dismissed any notion that he might try to bargain for his own life at the expense of the lives of the people. On July 22, 1979, he repeated an earlier assertion that "the shepherd does not want security while they give no security to his flock." Such solidarity with the people endeared him to them all the more, and crowds flocked to hear him, whether in person or through the diocesan radio station. Eventually, the station itself was sabotaged as a way to silence him. But still Romero was unruffled, reminding the people that he had always predicted this possibility and that they themselves had to become loudspeakers broadcasting the gospel in the face of any opposition. And as the threats against him increased, he continued to assure all who looked to him "that I will not abandon my people, but together with them I will run all the risks that my ministry demands."[13]

Things came to a head at the start of the new year, the beginning of a new decade. In the early part of 1980, Romero spoke directly to those serving in the military. Reminding them that no soldier is obliged to obey an order that goes against God's law, he contended that their unquestioning obedience to the unreasonable, immoral orders of their superiors had resulted in the deaths of their own people. They were torturing and killing their Salvadoran brothers and sisters. In the film *Romero*, we see him speak of the situation as "an abomination," directly addressing the members of the armed forces in the most forceful way: "In the name of God, in the name of this suffering people whose cry rises to heaven more loudly each day, I implore you, I beg you, I order you: Stop the repression!" With these words, Romero had all but signed his own death sentence.

On March 24, 1980, in a small chapel near his cathedral, while lifting up the chalice as he consecrated Holy Communion, Archbishop Oscar Romero was shot dead, most likely by a member of a Salvadoran death squad. The murder shocked the world. Not since Thomas à Becket's murder in 1170 by soldiers of King Henry II in Canterbury Cathedral had such a heinous act occurred. But unlike Becket's murder, this time there was no king who begged God's pardon. Instead, the repression continued, with more than sixty thousand Salvadorans killed over the coming decade. Indeed, as recently as 2010, thirty years after Romero's death, there was a failed assassination attempt on the life of the Anglican archbishop of El Salvador.

Though there has been quiet resistance on the part of some in the Roman Catholic Church hierarchy about pursuing the process of canonization to name Romero a saint, Anglicans embraced him as a saint and martyr almost immediately, with the Church of England unveiling a statue of him on the west door of Westminster Abbey in London, as part of a larger tribute to ten twentieth-century martyrs. Likewise, both the Church of England and the Episcopal Church in the United States have marked March 24 in their liturgical calendars as his commemoration date, and the latter has further included him in a publication on saints' feast days, *Holy Women, Holy Men*.[14]

DEALING WITH DANGER

Romero's assassination was tragic and yet—though he was unaware of the time and place—he went to his death fully prepared. Somewhere in those years following Grande's murder, the formerly conflict-averse prelate had discovered a faith and courage that was stronger than his fears and his opponents' threats. He had uncovered the depth of a pastor's love that was always present, but somehow previously dormant. But when the fires in him were ignited, they shone brightly for all to see. And far from extinguishing those flames, Romero's death simply spread his message further and made his legacy greater. He had been clear with all who would hear him, both friend and foe alike, that to be committed to the poor meant being willing to suffer their fate, which in El Salvador at that time often meant torture and death. But even if a bishop should die, Romero knew that the Church, the communion of Jesus's faithful people, would live on. It had to, for there was still work to accomplish, with or without Romero's leadership. In his last homily, only minutes before his assassination, Archbishop Oscar Romero reminded his cathedral congregation that "every effort to better society, especially when injustice and sin are so ingrained, is an effort that God blesses, that God wants, that God demands of us."[15] There had been many in leadership in the nation and even in parts of the Church who wanted Romero to be silent, and others who wanted him to rise up in violence. But like Jesus, whom he so faithfully served, Romero sought a different way and made the violence of love the only kind of violence he would espouse.

For Reflection

1. In the movie of Romero's life, it is easy to see his reluctance to stir up trouble. Only after the murder of his friend, Father Grande, did he find the courage to speak up. What has kept you from speaking up in the past?

2. Romero called his opponents to repent and be forgiven, a tall order when one considers the oppression they enforced. When is it appropriate for soldiers and others under authority to say "no" and go against their superiors?

3. Janani Luwum and Oscar Romero were contemporaries of one another. What similarities do you see in them, and what differences?

4. What does the phrase "the violence of love" mean to you? Is it real ... or realistic?

For Further Reading

Brockman, James R. *Romero: A Life*. 25th ed. Maryknoll, NY: Orbis Books, 2005.

Dennis, Marie, Renny Golden, and Scott Wright. *Oscar Romero: Reflections on His Life and Writings*. Maryknoll, NY: Orbis Books, 2000.

Romero, Oscar. *The Violence of Love*. Translated by James R. Brockman. Maryknoll, NY: Orbis Books, 2004.

———. *Voice of the Voiceless: The Four Pastoral Letters and Other Statements*. Translated by Michael J. Walsh. Maryknoll, NY: Orbis Books, 1985.

For an inspiring and accurate film portrayal of Romero's time as archbishop, see *Romero*. DVD. Directed by John Duigan and starring Raul Julia. Worcester, PA: Vision Video, 2009.

12

K. H. TING

The Reconstructionist

I will be very happy if I am remembered as one who
has had something to do with running the Church well.

—K. H. TING, IN A 1996
INTERVIEW WITH *AREOPAGUS*

He is one of the most controversial Christian leaders in the
past century, the man from Shanghai who uttered those
seemingly innocent and even parochial words. But there is nothing
parochial—and, some would add, innocent—about K. H. Ting.
Indeed, throughout his long life Ting has proved to be something
of a lightning rod. So much of the controversy has to do with the
way his life and his theology were interwoven with political and
social changes in twentieth-century China, including the National
Salvation Movement during the Japanese occupation, the establishment of the Three-Self Patriotic Movement, and most notably,
the rise of the Chinese Communist Party. Despite this, it is difficult to overstate Ting's wide-ranging contributions to the Christian
faith, mission, and ecumenical witness in China. For Ting, the

focus was clear. He sought a "new and healthy Christianity with Chinese characteristics." It is the practical implications of this seemingly simple notion that would make him, to some, a revered living symbol of Christian faithfulness and, to others, a very dangerous man.

To Be a Christian in China

From Ting's birth in 1915, Shanghai was his home. It was also home to millions of others, earning it the rank of sixth-largest city in the world. The city's international settlement, where Ting was born, was the address for Japanese, British, American, and many other expatriates, bankers, diplomats, industrialists, and missionaries. Like other Chinese living in this part of Shanghai, Ting grew up familiar with the foreigners and their ways. It also meant that he and his family saw the effects of foreign occupation up close and even had to evacuate the city when it grew too dangerous with the Japanese occupation. He was the third of four children born to Ding Chufan, a mid-level manager, and Li Jinglan, a devout Christian whose own father was one of the first clergy in the Episcopal Church in China, having served in his lifetime at St. Peter's Church, the same church where Ting and his brothers and sister were baptized and the family worshipped. To Ting's mother, he was Bao Bao, or "precious," and her influence on his life, his self-esteem, and his faith were considerable. The same could not be said about Ting's father, with whom he would have a severely strained relationship throughout his life, at least in part because of Ting's choice to seek ordination instead of pursuing a more lucrative and respectable vocation such as engineering or medicine. From his mother, Ting gained both a deep appreciation of scripture and a reasonable approach to faith that avoided emotional extremes. At home, Bible study and worship were a regular part of family life. Ting's later theological expressions of the love of God being like that of a mother undoubtedly are grounded in the love and nurturing formation he experienced as a child from Li Jinglan.

St. Peter's Church also proved to be a formidable influence on Ting. It was one of the few truly self-supporting churches in early twentieth-century China, a remarkable fact given the many expressions of various missionary movements active in China at the time. At St. Peter's, Ting grew up in a church that had Chinese clergy, Chinese members, and Chinese concerns. Unlike the missionaries and missionary churches that showed little interest in the internal political and social realities of China, the clergy at St. Peter's displayed strong progressive leanings and often allowed socialist groups to meet in their facilities. Ironically, St. John's University in Shanghai, where Ting spent his college years, was still under missionary leadership, and courses were all taught in English. Ting struggled with the apparent disconnect between what he experienced at seminary and what was going on all around him. In light of the incursions into regions of China by the neighboring island nation of Japan, more and more students were asking hard questions about the role of the Church in matters of national identity. In return, they received what they deemed to be unsatisfactory answers from foreign missionaries. By senior year, Ting was disillusioned with the Church and put aside his ordination plans, instead taking up work with the YMCA, which was heavily involved in the growing student political movement.

To understand more clearly the frustrations that Ting and other Chinese Christians felt, it is important to step back in time and understand something of the history of the faith in China. Although Christians had established places of worship as early as the seventh century, it was centuries later, during the Mongol Empire, that the faith exerted a significant impact. This was an Eastern form of the Christian faith, not connected to Rome and the pope. When Western Christianity did come to China, it was initially through Franciscan missionaries in the late thirteenth century, and it was not long before they were cast out, as the Ming Dynasty warned against the dangers of foreign influences, including religions like Christianity and Buddhism. In the sixteenth century, Jesuit missionaries appeared, bringing with them not only the faith but Western ideas, education, science, and language.

The warnings from the Ming Dynasty eventually came to pass, during a conflict in the early eighteenth century that became known as the Chinese Rites controversy. The pope declared that the folk rituals and offerings to ancestors practiced by Chinese Christians—which were not known or understood by Westerners—were pagan practices and would not be tolerated by the Church. In essence, the unfamiliar was declared unacceptable. The Chinese emperor retaliated as emperors before him had done, by banning the foreign Christian incursion. In the nineteenth century, following the First Opium War, Protestant missionaries entered China and contributed further to the Westernization of the country. One of the more interesting effects of their early efforts was the Taiping Rebellion, a Chinese civil war led by a convert of the missionaries, Hong Xiuquan. He embraced a very peculiar form of Christianity, claiming to be the younger brother of Jesus and demanding that his followers supplant traditional expressions of faith, such as Confucianism and Chinese folk religions. Overseeing an army of ethnic minorities, Hong initiated a fourteen-year conflict, the last few years coinciding with the American Civil War. This was total war, with casualties including countless civilian lives. The death toll made it one of the deadliest wars of the nineteenth century. Interestingly, a century later, Chairman Mao spoke of the Taiping Rebellion as a kind of proto-Communist movement. But for many, Hong Xiuquan's bizarre, and ultimately deadly, version of the faith meant one more reason not to trust foreign missionaries.

By Ting's own time, the missionary movement had reached remarkable heights, with as many as eight thousand Protestant foreign missionaries in China by 1925. The China Inland Mission, the largest such agency in the country, initiated by the famous Brethren missionary J. Hudson Taylor, actually spoke of the goal of an indigenous Chinese Church that was independent of foreign control. This goal was not shared by the majority of mission agencies, who instead boasted that Western progress was in large part due to the Christian heritage of the West. These missionaries brought with them, therefore, both the faith and their familiar Western culture, never imagining that there could be a different form of Christianity in a different cultural context. Many of their contributions were positive, such as breakthroughs in medical knowledge and techniques, as well as schools that often provided the only educational opportunity available for Chinese children from poor families before the coming of the Chinese Republic. Christian organizations such as the YMCA and YWCA also flourished, though they became known more for their political, and not strictly religious, aims. And then, of course, there were the evangelical and Pentecostal groups. In the midst of this explosion of Christianity, many Chinese questioned not so much the faith, but rather the assumption that the faith, as well as the so-called progress associated with it, could only be obtained through foreign influence and foreign control. Some began to ask what an indigenous Chinese Christianity might actually look like.

Ting did eventually agree to ordination, partly because of the influence of Christians like Y. T. Wu, an outspoken leader in the National Salvation Movement during the years of Japanese occupation. For Ting, Wu represented something new, something he had not seen in the kind of faith represented by the foreign missionaries. As he later wrote, Ting was impressed with the ways in which Wu's "love for Christ and his concern for the well-being of the people were harmonized."[1] More to the point, Wu saw little problem in "harmonizing" his Christian faith with the growing interest in Communism in China and became a major advocate for the Communists' approach to needed change in the country. Ting would indeed be both inspired and influenced by Wu, although he also later admitted a "little distance" between Wu and himself, mostly because Ting came to believe that the emphasis had to be on Christian faith first, then on the political party, while Wu reversed the order.

It is important once again to underscore how much of Ting's openness to the rise of Communism was at least in part the result of hardships the Chinese experienced in the nineteenth and early twentieth centuries. Japan's invasion of Manchuria and eventual occupation of much of China reinforced Chinese dreams of "national salvation," and student groups in particular led the way in seeking autonomy for the country and a united front against all forms of imperialism and outside aggression. By the time World War II ended, China was anything but united, as civil war engulfed the country, with the divide between Nationalists and Communists particularly great in an urban center like Shanghai. For Ting and others, Communism was not evil, but a valid choice closer to gospel truths than the "imperialism" and unbridled capitalism they witnessed in Japan and other foreign countries. Ting himself wanted to embrace a kind of Christianity that helped "people exalt justice, enhance moral sense, and distinguish right from wrong."[2] He believed this was found most clearly in an indigenous, socialist form of faith and political thought. For this reason, he eventually became a leader in the Three-Self Patriotic Movement (TSPM), initiated by Wu and emphasizing self-governance, self-support (financial), and self-propagation (in terms of rejecting the need for foreign missionaries). It was this movement that allowed the Christian faith to continue in an official capacity up until the Cultural Revolution, while other independent forms of the faith, usually either Pentecostal or evangelical, were often banned.

As for Ting, his involvement in organizations like the YMCA, the Student Christian Movement, and the TSPM was consistent with his belief that theology and faith were not at all in opposition with participation in political and social issues. Although an Anglican priest, he was less attracted to dogmatic (and inherently Western, to his viewpoint) theological formulas, such as the Thirty-Nine Articles of the Anglican Church, and more to an emphasis on the Incarnation and Trinity, the connection between creation and redemption, a critical approach to scripture, and the end of denominationalism. In the decades to come, Ting would interweave his theology with a loyalty to his motherland and trust in Communism's principles. This combination made him a controversial ambassador for Chinese Christianity.

Days of Persecution

Having lived in Shanghai during the Japanese occupation, Ting had understandable antipathy for anything he saw as foreign imperialism. With the close of World War II, China finally experienced freedom from Japan, but it was followed by civil war. The Nationalists and the Communists were vying for power, even as Ting was watching from afar while working with the Student Christian Movement in Canada. During his years abroad, Ting strengthened ecumenical ties and developed a clearer sense of what he termed "expectant evangelism," arguing that the established Church in the West had become complacent and the so-called new churches remained unclear about what it meant to be evangelists themselves, instead relying on foreign missionaries to do their work for them. Evangelism, he said, was at the core of what it means to be Christian: "If Christ has become anything to you, he must be everything to you. And if indeed he is everything to you, how anxious you must be that he should be everything to all people everywhere."[3] Part of this evangelistic work, Ting asserted, was cooperating with God in extending the "new humanity" in which the Church would take root in culture and people would be transformed in the here and now, not simply in heaven. This merging of an evangelistic mission with what many call the social gospel was a critical component in Ting's theology, opening him up to charges of being too optimistic about the human ability for change. For Ting, however, this "partnership in obedience" was simply the natural outgrowth of believing in a God who acts in human history as proclaimed in the scriptures and ultimately made evident in the Incarnation—God's becoming human in the person of Jesus.

By the time Ting and his family returned to China in the early 1950s, change had already taken place, spearheaded not by the Church but by the Communists, whose revolution was bringing about a "New China." The premier of China, Zhou Enlai, met with Y. T. Wu and other Chinese Christian leaders at the outbreak of the Korean War, urging them to cut ties with foreign missionaries and instead do reforming work in the Church themselves. Wu and others penned a "Chinese Manifesto," which spoke of support for the new government and partnership in building a New China. Ting's role in all this is difficult to assess, for while he returned to China against friends' pleas, he did not sign the manifesto.

Indeed, Ting's role in much of what would come is difficult to pin down. He did not share the perspective of many of the more radical members of the Three-Self Patriotic Movement who supported the "Denunciation Movement," in which foreign missionaries were accused and ejected from China for allegedly bringing with them imperialistic ways. Years later, he went so far as to say that the movement "hurt many people and damaged our international reputation."[4] And yet Ting remained a loyal and increasingly influential member of the TSPM, many of whose members did participate in the Denunciation Movement. He continued to view things through theological rather than political lenses, though his patriotism was never in question even when others were being imprisoned. Indeed, he cited the Bible to challenge the views of those whom he believed were not concerned with China and its internal affairs. Ting appears to have merged his patriotism with pragmatism, doing what he could to support the new government, but always from a Christian platform. He soon was selected to head up the newly formed Nanjing Union Theological Seminary, a training institution for pastors that replaced previously independent seminaries and brought together in one place Christian leaders of different theological persuasions. As lecturer, writer, and seminary head, Ting thrived—but that was not the case for other Christian leaders who refused to embrace the new government.

Wang Mingdao, Sung Shangjie (John Sung), and Ni Tuosheng (Watchman Nee) were the most prominent independent Christian leaders who eventually faced imprisonment in the 1950s for being part of "counterrevolutionary cliques." To their followers, they provided uncompromising faith in the face of a culture that was in great flux. Westerners hearing vague reports of the persecution from outside looked at figures like Wang and Nee and deemed them modern martyrs, although their own sectarian beliefs were more questionable than many in the West would at times admit. Nee, a prolific writer whose books and articles fill volumes, never studied at a seminary or Bible school, but instead soaked up everything he could from several influential persons in his life, beginning with his mother, a devout believer who was responsible for his name change to "the bell ringer" or "watchman." His other mentors were largely women who came out of sectarian traditions and from whom he developed an eclectic theology that included Pentecostal elements such as the emphasis on a "second baptism" and the gifts of the Spirit, apocalyptic elements such as belief in a "partial rapture" and a kind of purgatory, and other more unusual elements such as his insistence of "recovery" truth through his divinely endowed visions.

Nee, Wang, Sung, and others like them resisted not only the Communist regime but also any notion of the validity of existing churches, whether Roman Catholic or Protestant. They were largely exclusivists who had little desire to engage in the kind of "mutual respect" that Ting believed to be crucial for Chinese believers. Nee advocated the principle of one church per city, which of course meant one of his house churches, which he termed the "Little Flock." Although he drew upon Plymouth Brethren principles of what it means to be a church, in fact Nee (as well as Wang and other similar leaders) operated on a fairly authoritarian level, with his word, supported by his visions from God, providing the last word. This tendency continued with his successor, Witness Lee, who developed a global organization complete with its own publishing arm, through which Nee's books have been promulgated through the years. In recent times, Witness Lee and his Living Stream movement have been challenged by dozens of leading evangelical scholars for questionable and potentially heretical teachings about the Trinity, scripture, and the Church, as well as for the substantial number of lawsuits in which they have been engaged. Others have spoken out in their defense. In any case, one could rightly argue that this is not Watchman Nee's fault, though the roots of such problems are evident in Nee's own teachings.

All of this is to say that figures like Nee and Wang were perhaps more controversial than their followers and Western believers would paint them to be. However, what is undeniably true—and unconscionable—is that these leaders and many other "underground" Christians with them were imprisoned for years and eventually died as a result of their hardships. And Ting and others with him either said nothing or actually supported such moves against those who were not supportive of the "reforming" efforts of the government. It was during this period that Ting actually began to speak less about his faith and instead became a more visible advocate of the "high tide of socialism." Like others, Ting appears to have naively believed that Chairman Mao, who now ruled China and overshadowed Zhou Enlai, had every intention of continuing to support the Church as long as it proved loyal to China's government. The turning point for Ting, as for many intellectuals, was of course the stark reality that came crashing down on all of China during the period from 1966 to 1976 that would become known as the Cultural Revolution.

No one could have predicted the devastation, the destruction, and the violence of that dark period of Chinese history. Young students established themselves as "Red Guards" and "made revolution," pillaging and killing anyone they believed held on to the "Four Olds," namely old ideas, old culture, old customs, old habits. Because these young people chanted Mao's name and slogans, he thought he could control them, especially as his wife, Jiang Qing, was a leading instigator of the Cultural Revolution. Instead, it became a time of anarchy. Order only began to come about with the arrival of the People's Liberation Army, and even then it would be a few more years before peace finally came once more to China and people could sing, "The winter is past, the rain is o'er" (Song of Solomon 2:11).

In the midst of the violence, almost everyone associated with Christianity was either imprisoned, killed, or put to work on labor farms or in rural communities where they could be "rehabilitated." Churches were shut down, converted for other uses, or destroyed. Not even the Tings were immune to the chaos, as they were forced to evacuate their home as Red Guards entered Shanghai, and the two were separated for some time as Ting was taken off under guard to a northern rural area far from home. Ting's wife, Siu-May Kuo, suffered humiliations and deprivations but appears to have escaped any outright abuse. Ting himself avoided prison and death, some say as a result of the quiet intervention of the nearby Anglican bishop of Hong Kong, while others claim the more plausible reason was the direct protection of Zhou Enlai, who had befriended Ting and always supported his desire for a Christian "united front" in line with the government, not a threat to it. Friends and colleagues were not so fortunate, and Ting took notice of people he knew to be innocent suddenly accused of crimes against the state. Even with some outside protection, Ting himself was suspect, chiefly because of earlier writings, especially an essay titled "On Christian Theism." In any case, whatever naiveté Ting had in the 1950s, when Wang and Nee were persecuted, and even in the early years of the Cultural Revolution, when he himself was "rehabilitated," it was long gone by the end of that decade of troubles. When asked later what aspect of faith he came to understand more deeply in that dark period, Ting immediately responded, "Resurrection!"[5]

RECONSTRUCTING CHRISTIANITY

Following the chaos of the Cultural Revolution, Ting devoted his efforts first to the restoration and expansion of religious liberty, then to the reconstruction of Chinese Christianity. Noting that during the Cultural Revolution Christian churches were closed and people had to meet secretly in homes for worship, he argued for the legality of such house churches: "In interpreting the constitution, we cannot say that there is religious freedom in church buildings but not in homes."[6] This was an extraordinary move from Ting's earlier suspicion of the "ultra-right," but the excesses of the Cultural Revolution now gave him a voice to criticize the "ultra-left." Without articulating it as such, he was seeking an almost Anglican middle way that allowed for the mutual respect he had always desired. Robert Runcie, archbishop of Canterbury, invited him to the Lambeth Conference of Anglican bishops in 1988, speaking of Ting as "an Anglican plus something." Ting went on to head both the TSPM and the newly formed China Christian Council (CCC) and was viewed more and more as chief ambassador for Chinese Christians.

In the midst of this, Ting also called for reconstruction of the faith in China on several levels. Financially, he called on Chinese Christians to avoid returning to times past when they relied on foreign intervention coupled with foreign control. As head of

Nanjing Seminary, he pushed for the recruitment and training of young Chinese Christian leaders. On the ecumenical front, he fought for the inclusion of the China Christian Council in the World Council of Churches. With the creation of the Amity Foundation, an independent voluntary organization promoting Chinese social development and openness to the outside world and cross-cultural dialogue, Ting promoted several projects such as a teachers program and Bible printing. He also encouraged greater theological pluralism and stood against the kind of exclusivist fundamentalism he had always feared. At a TSPM/CCC Joint Standing Committee meeting in 1995, he argued that "there are many doctrines in Christianity besides justification by faith"[7] and went on to list some of those that he counted as key tenets of Christian faith: the Incarnation and resurrection; the renewal of creation; the indwelling of the Holy Spirit, which bestows wisdom; the Beatitudes; the Great Commandment; the Golden Rule. He echoed St. Paul the Apostle's assertion that love, not faith, is the highest virtue, and argued that God's will cannot be endless divisions.

Having said his farewell to his beloved wife of fifty-three years, Siu-May Kuo, who died in 1995, Ting has pressed on alone into the new millennium with his ongoing work of trying to help run the Church well. To those who revere Chinese independent leaders of times past like Watchman Nee, Ting is viewed with great suspicion or even outright antagonism as one who sold out to the government. To others, he is the living embodiment of Christian perseverance, making his way through times of change and revolution with pragmatism and grace. This author had the opportunity to meet K. H. Ting on a visit to China in 2008. Though frail and wheelchair-bound, Ting still showed the same passion that he always displayed, coupled with good humor and an awareness that God is larger than any of us. As one observer noted, there was both a fire and a twinkle in Ting's eyes.

DEALING WITH DANGER

There is no doubt that K. H. Ting was, and remains, an important though ambiguous Christian leader. While other Christians have been viewed as dangerous in their time because they stood up to their governments, Ting has been viewed with suspicion because of his willingness to work with, instead of against, his government. But for those who are quick to critique him for linking Christianity with Communism, Ting himself might well turn the challenge around, gently asking whether we have not done a similar thing in the West, and particularly in the United States, often wrapping the cross in the American flag. While it is indeed a tragic fact that the Denunciation Movement in 1950s China meant the destruction of reputations and even imprisonment for those considered ultra-right, the fact remains that during that same decade, Senator Joseph McCarthy and the House Un-American Activities Committee conducted veritable witch hunts for suspected Communists in the United States. And both before and since, we have had sad situations of violence and bigotry against racial and ethnic minorities. The difference, of course, is in degree. Chairman Mao was a tyrant, and under him, China became a closed society. We in the West are blessed to be able to critique and criticize our government and its policies. Winston Churchill once wisely said that democracy is the worst form of government, except for all the rest. Mao himself, in his earlier days as a guerilla leader, when asked if Communism had found a way to break the usual cycle of dynastic rule and decay, responded, "We have found a way; it's called democracy." If only he had lived according to those words. Instead, under him, China experienced the horrors of the Cultural Revolution. We who live in the West are indeed blessed to be in a system that celebrates individual liberty. But the fact remains that Christianity can never be fully synonymous with any socioeconomic or political system, whether it is capitalism or Communism.

Ting pointed out the pride that some foreigners brought with them into China that people in the West know what is best not only for themselves but for everyone else. That pride, he might well argue, prevents not only mutual respect, but true mutual learning. Having at one time been suspect himself by the ultra-left, Ting might well warn against judging anyone else too quickly and instead call for all Christians to "agree to differ and resolve to love."[8] In this way, Ting has tried to show that the way to follow Jesus is not in exclusivist claims to being right while all others are wrong, but rather in doing what Jesus did and listening to what he said. It is how we live with one another, Ting might well say, that is the best advertisement to the world of what we believe. He might well echo the words attributed to Francis of Assisi, "Preach the Gospel at all times; if necessary, use words."[9]

For many in the West, the jury is still out on K. H. Ting, but there is no debate that he has been a key player in reconstructing indigenous Christianity in China. And perhaps he is most dangerous to those of us who are so familiar with our own systems that we have difficulty looking beyond them.

For Reflection

1. K. H. Ting has proved himself to be loyal to his country, while also being willing to criticize it and its excesses. What do you love about your country, and what would you like to see changed or improved in it?

2. Ting has continually emphasized the need to work in and with society, while other Chinese evangelists have at times focused almost exclusively on preparation of the soul for heaven. What do you think is the right balance? What does it mean to live for Jesus in the here and now while also keeping sight of eternity?

3. Ting has repeatedly insisted on the importance of "running the church well." What does this mean to you? What does a church "run well" say about the gospel we proclaim to the world?

For Further Reading

Ting, K. H. *God Is Love: Collected Writings of Bishop K. H. Ting*. Colorado Springs, CO: Cook Communications Ministries International, 2004.

Whitehead, Raymond L., ed. *No Longer Strangers: Selected Writings of K. H. Ting*. Maryknoll, NY: Orbis Books, 1989.

Wickeri, Janice, ed. *Love Never Ends: Papers by K. H. Ting*. Jiangsu Province, China: Yilin Press, 2000.

Wickeri, Philip L. *Reconstructing Christianity in China: K. H. Ting and the Chinese Church*. Maryknoll, NY: Orbis Books, 2007.

EPILOGUE

These are they who have come out of the
great ordeal; they have washed their robes
and made them white in the blood of the
Lamb.

—REVELATION 7:14

"Wait, what about...?" Each time that I tell friends (or
strangers who will listen to me, for that matter) the title
of this book, they immediately ask who I included among this
dangerous dozen. As I run through the list, inevitably they nod at
some names but look perplexed at others, asking why someone else
was not chosen instead. It is a valid question. Why not include
John Chrysostom or Martin Luther or Rosa Parks or any number
of other Christians who have similarly challenged the status quo?
It's true that this has been a subjective enterprise, but it could not
be otherwise. But there were some important criteria to which I
alluded in the introduction but should spell out here.

First, some choices are obvious to me, and judging from
friends' (and patient strangers') nods, they are obvious to others as
well. It would be impossible to write such a book about Christians

who challenged the status quo without including the Apostle Paul and Francis of Assisi. This entire project, in fact, was born out of a conversation with my editor over lunch when I told her about a class I once taught on Paul and Francis titled "Two Dangerous Men." When the book was conceived as a way of highlighting others like them, there were a few more names that seemed to be fairly obvious: Dietrich Bonhoeffer and Oscar Romero. The latter in particular happens to be a personal hero of mine, ever since I first saw the late Raul Julia portray the Salvadorian archbishop in a film produced by a dear friend and colleague of mine, Michael Rhodes. I knew Romero had to be in this book.

Then there were others who made their way in who, though they were not quite so obvious at first, upon further reflection made perfect sense. Dorothy Day comes to mind. Having always heard her name, I never truly explored who she was until another film by Michael Rhodes, this time directed by him, introduced me to this remarkable social activist. Dorothy Day also kept this from becoming some kind of men's-only club. I immediately thought about someone who was as seminal a figure in the early Church as Paul, but even more threatening because of her gender—the enigmatic Mary Magdalene. I almost did not include Mary precisely because she has been featured in so many recent books and even movies. But because she has not always been treated with accuracy, I decided it was well worth including her here.

There were others who appeared to be obvious choices at first but in the end didn't make the cut. These include Martin Luther and Martin Luther King Jr., both renowned Christians who clearly transformed the world. But so much has been written about both of them that I decided to consider others a little less well known who could convey the specific period (the Reformation, in Luther's case) or specific struggle (equal rights for African Americans, in King's case) that I wanted to share. This led me respectively to Thomas Cranmer, who did make it in, and Rosa Parks, who did not. As I researched Parks, I was suddenly aware of how many individuals I had from the twentieth century and decided to see if there was someone of comparable impact in the nineteenth century instead. It was through this circuitous route that I discovered Sojourner Truth, whose name was far more familiar to me than her story, but who ended up being one of my personal favorites. The other person I wanted to include but did not was Larry Norman, the living symbol of the Jesus Movement in post-1960s religious America and described as the father of Christian rock. However, I finally said no to Norman because I realized I wanted to expand the geographic boundaries beyond the West.

It was the desire to look beyond my own culture that led me to two of the lesser-known, but perhaps most intriguing, figures in the book, Janani Luwum of Uganda and K. H. Ting of China. Both were surrounded by controversy—Ting especially—but it is their edginess that made them even more attractive to me as figures to include. It may well be that history eventually leads others to different opinions of either person, but there is no debating the fact that both have left a considerable mark on the Church and society in their respective contexts. Both have been dangerous forces in their own worlds.

I also wanted to go back through time a little more and do some more digging into the past. So I decided to look at Hildegard and Origen. With both of these characters, I found that the years melted away as I discovered to my utter delight that there was so much about each of them to which I could relate in the twenty-first century. In the end, all the members of this dangerous dozen were salt and light in their own times and their own contexts. Although some of those who made this list enjoyed approval by Church and state in their own lifetimes, many instead faced their own "great ordeal" as martyrs following in the way of the cross. All ultimately should be included among those "robed in white" as described in the book of Revelation.

Before saying goodbye to all these agents of transformation, I would like to add one more story, a personal one, about the contributor of this book's foreword. I first met Desmond Tutu on the campus of Emory University, when he was teaching there while on sabbatical. I came upon him quite by accident as I was on my way to guest-lecture, and he was leaving for the day, accompanied by a very large companion who I can only call his handler. I ran up to introduce myself, only to be stopped in my tracks by his companion with the proclamation, "The archbishop is busy." Well, I certainly felt like chopped liver, and I nodded and quietly turned to walk away. But I heard a gentle voice say, "Come, come." As I turned back to him, beaming, I heard him say, "Tell me your name." I stammered, but got it out. "So tell me about yourself, Chuck Robertson." For the next ten or fifteen minutes, I told him about who I was and what I was doing. And this remarkable man, who had changed the world and met any number of dignitaries and celebrities, now focused all his attention on me. On me! Time stood still for those minutes, and I felt like the most important person in the world. As the time passed and I prepared to leave, he put a hand on my shoulder and said, "I will remember you, Chuck Robertson."

I share this story because it reminds me that sometimes we as Christians do not have to challenge the status quo of Church and society in order to make a difference. Sometimes we do it simply by touching one other life and helping someone know that she or he is God's beloved. Desmond Tutu is in so many ways an inspiration, to be included alongside many of the people in these pages. But what most astounds me is that he also is a fellow pilgrim who could see the face of Jesus in my face. And that is a gift I want to pass on to others.

Notes

PROLOGUE: THE OUTLAW

1. Saint Francis of Assisi, "Legend of Perugia," in *Saint Francis of Assisi: Writings and Early Biographies, Omnibus of Sources,* vol. 2 (San Jose, CA: Franciscan Press, 1991).

2. Robert Ellsberg, ed., *Dorothy Day: Selected Writings* (Maryknoll, NY: Orbis, 2005), xxvii.

3. Fyodor Dostoevsky, *The Brothers Karamazov,* Bantam Classics Edition (New York: Bantam, 1984).

PAUL OF TARSUS: THE CATALYST

1. Marcus Aurelius Antoninus, *The Meditations of the Emperor Marcus Aurelius Antoninus,* trans. Francis Hutcheson (Indianapolis: Liberty Fund, 2008), 6:54.

MARY MAGDALENE: THE WITNESS

1. Marvin Meyer and James Robinson, eds., *The Nag Hammadi Library,* rev. ed. (New York: HarperCollins, 1990), 308.

2. G. R. S. Mead, *Pistis Sophia: A Gnostic Gospel,* rev. ed. (San Diego: The Book Tree, 2006), 259.

3. Meyer and Robinson, *Nag Hammadi Library,* 167.

4. Ibid., 171.

5. Stevan Davies, trans., *The Gospel of Thomas: Annotated & Explained* (Woodstock, VT: SkyLight Paths, 2002), 139.

6. Meyer and Robinson, *Nag Hammadi Library,* 743. Also see Karen King, *The Gospel of Mary of Magdala* (Salem, OR: Polebridge Press, 2003).

7. Meyer and Robinson, *Nag Hammadi Library,* 745.

8. Ibid.

ORIGEN OF ALEXANDRIA: THE INNOVATOR

1. *On First Principles*, 1.8.2.
2. Ibid.
2. Ibid., 1.5.2.
3. Ibid.

FRANCIS OF ASSISI: THE RADICAL

1. Paul Sabatier, *The Road to Assisi: The Essential Biography of St. Francis*, ed. Jon M. Sweeney (Orleans, MA: Paraclete Press, 2004), 49.
2. See his "Canticle of Brother Sun."

HILDEGARD OF BINGEN: THE VISIONARY

1. Hildegard of Bingen, "Letter to Bernard," in *Hildegard of Bingen: Selected Writings,* trans. Mark Atherton (New York: Penguin, 2001), 5.
2. Ibid., 3.
3. Marshall McLuhan, *Understanding Media: The Extensions of Man* (Corte Madera, CA: Gingko Press, 2003), 8.
4. Hildegard of Bingen, "Letter to Pope Eugenius III," in *Hildegard of Bingen*, 32.
5. Ibid.
6. Ibid., 66.
7. Ibid.
8. Ibid.
9. Hildegard of Bingen, "Letter to Pope Hadrian IV," in *Hildegard of Bingen*, 68.
10. Hildegard of Bingen, "The Iron Mountain," in *Hildegard of Bingen*, 134.
11. Hildegard of Bingen, "Letter to Bishop of Liege," in *Hildegard of Bingen*, 67.
12. From the Introduction, *Hildegard of Bingen*, xv.
13. From the letter of Pope Gregory IX, cited within the Canonization Protocol, in *Hildegard of Bingen*, 197.
14. Hildegard of Bingen, "The Book of Divine Works," 1.1.2, in *Hildegard of Bingen*, 172.
15. See the Introduction in *Hildegard of Bingen*, xxxv.

THOMAS CRANMER: THE REFORMER

1. Felix Pryor, *Elizabeth I: Her Life in Letters* (Berkeley, CA: University of California Press, 2003), 29.
2. Book of Common Prayer, 1979 American Edition, Collect 28, 236.

3. Peter Newman Brooks, *Cranmer in Context: Documents from the English Reformation* (Minneapolis: Fortress Press, 1989), 100.

4. Diarmaid MacCullough, *Thomas Cranmer: A Life* (New Haven, CT: Yale University Press, 1996), 573.

5. Brooks, *Cranmer in Context*, 97.

6. Ibid., 116.

7. Ibid.

Sojourner Truth: The Liberator

1. Introduction to *Narrative of Sojourner Truth*, ed. Margaret Washington (New York: Vintage, 1993), x.

2. "Libyan Sybil," in *Narrative of Sojourner Truth*, xi.

3. *Narrative of Sojourner Truth*, xxviii.

4. Ibid., xxix.

5. Ibid., 15.

6. Ibid., 24.

7. Ibid., 29.

8. Ibid., 50.

9. Ibid., 51.

10. Ibid., 80.

11. Ibid., 101.

12. "Ain't I a Woman?" in *Narrative of Sojourner Truth*, 118.

13. *Narrative of Sojourner Truth*, 80.

14. Ibid., 87

15. Ibid.

16. Ibid., 89.

Dorothy Day: The Activist

1. Dorothy Day, *Dorothy Day: Selected Writings* (Maryknoll, NY: Orbis Books, 20056), xxiv.

2. Ibid., xxv.

3. From the film *Entertaining Angels: The Dorothy Day Story*, DVD, directed by Michael Rhodes (Clinton, NY: Vision Video, 1996).

4. *Dorothy Day: Selected Writings*, xxxi.

5. Dorothy Day, *The Long Loneliness: The Autobiography of the Legendary Catholic Social Activist* (New York: HarperOne, 1996).

6. *Dorothy Day: Selected Writings*, 199.

7. Ibid., 104.

8. Ibid., 96.

9. Ibid., xli.

10. Robert Ellsberg, ed., *The Duty of Delight: The Diaries of Dorothy Day* (Milwaukee: Marquette University Press, 2008).

DIETRICH BONHOEFFER: THE RESISTER

1. Eberhard Bethge, *Dietrich Bonhoeffer: A Biography* (Minneapolis: Fortress, 2000), 36.

2. Elizabeth Raum, *Dietrich Bonhoeffer: Called by God* (New York: Continuum, 2003), 25.

3. Ibid., 47.

4. From "The Cost of Discipleship," in *Dietrich Bonhoeffer: Called by God*, 100.

5. Ibid.

6. Raum, *Dietrich Bonhoeffer*, 63.

7. Collected in Dietrich Bonhoeffer, *No Rusty Swords: Letters, Lectures, and Notes 1928–1936* (New York: Harper & Row, 1965), 226.

8. Raum, *Dietrich Bonhoeffer*, 75.

9. Ibid., 102.

10. Ibid., 100.

11. Ibid., 121.

12. Ibid., 124.

13. Dietrich Bonhoeffer, *Letters and Papers from Prison: An Abridged Edition* (Norwich, UK: SCM Press, 2001), 369.

14. Raum, *Dietrich Bonhoeffer*, 136.

15. Ibid., 146.

16. Ibid., 150.

17. Bonhoeffer, *Letters and Papers from Prison*, 347.

18. Raum, *Dietrich Bonhoeffer*, 140.

JANANI LUWUM: THE REVIVALIST

1. Luwum spoke these words on the day of his conversion, January 6, 1948, in his village of Acoli, Uganda.

2. Margaret Ford, *Janani: The Making of a Martyr* (New York: Harper & Row, 1978), 20.

3. Ibid., 23.

4. These words were spoken by U.S. Ambassador Thomas Patrick Melady in 1973.

5. George Every, Richard Harries, and Kalistos Ware, *The Time of the Spirit: Readings Through the Christian Year* (Yonkers, NY: St. Vladimir's Seminary Press, 1984), 113.

6. Ford, *Janani*, 49.

7. Ibid., 67.

8. Ibid., 74.

9. Ibid., 75.

10. See www.ucu.ac.ug/content/view/648/85.

11. Ford, *Janani*, 87.

OSCAR ROMERO: THE ADVOCATE

1. "Poverty of the Church," available online at www.shc.edu/theolibrary/resources/medpov.htm.

2. Ibid.

3. From Rutilio Grande's famed Apopa sermon, February 13, 1977, cited online at www.share-elsalvador.org/rutilio/091406a.htm.

4. From the film depiction of the archbishop's life, *Romero*, DVD, directed by John Duigan (Worcester, PA: Vision Video, 2009).

5. Oscar Romero, *The Violence of Love*, trans. James Brockman (New York: Harper & Row, 1988).

6. July 23, 1978 Speech, cited in Romero, *Violence of Love*, 80.

7. From a presentation Romero made in October 29, 1978, cited in Romero, *Violence of Love*, 118.

8. August 26, 1979, cited in Romero, *Violence of Love*, 172.

9. September 10, 1978, cited in Romero, *Violence of Love*, 100.

10. December 17, 1978, cited in Romero, *Violence of Love*, 123.

11. September 10, 1978, cited in Romero, *Violence of Love*, 102.

12. Ibid.

13. Spoken by Romero on November 11, 1979, cited in Romero, *Violence of Love*, 207.

14. *Holy Women, Holy Men: Celebrating the Saints* (New York: Church Publishing, 2009).

15. March 24, 1980, cited in Romero, *Violence of Love*, 219.

K. H. TING: THE RECONSTRUCTIONIST

1. Janice Wickeri, ed., *Love Never Ends: Papers by K. H. Ting* (Jiangsu Province, China: Yilin Press, 2000), 74.

2. From remarks Ting made at an August 2005 presentation in Hong Kong, cited in Philip L. Wickeri, *Reconstructing Christianity in China: K. H. Ting and the Chinese Church* (Maryknoll, NY: Orbis Books, 2007), 367.

3. Wickeri, *Reconstructing Christianity in China*, 86.

4. Ibid., 102.

5. Ibid., 194.

6. Ibid., 210.

7. Ibid., 343.

8. Ibid., 373.

9. The attribution of this quote to Francis is likely based on the seventeenth chapter of his Rule of 1221, where he urged his friars not to preach without proper permission from authorities and then added, "Let all the brothers, however, preach their deeds."

Spirituality

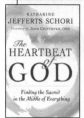

The Heartbeat of God: Finding the Sacred in the Middle of Everything
by Katharine Jefferts Schori; Foreword by Joan Chittister, OSB
Explores our connections to other people, to other nations and with the environment through the lens of faith. 6 x 9, 240 pp, HC, 978-1-59473-292-8 **$21.99**

A Dangerous Dozen: Twelve Christians Who Threatened the Status Quo but Taught Us to Live Like Jesus
by the Rev. Canon C. K. Robertson, PhD; Foreword by Archbishop Desmond Tutu
Profiles twelve visionary men and women who challenged society and showed the world a different way of living. 6 x 9, 208 pp, Quality PB, 978-1-59473-298-0 **$16.99**

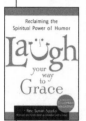

Laugh Your Way to Grace: Reclaiming the Spiritual Power of Humor
by Rev. Susan Sparks A powerful, humorous case for laughter as a spiritual, healing path. 6 x 9, 176 pp, Quality PB, 978-1-59473-280-5 **$16.99**

Living into Hope: A Call to Spiritual Action for Such a Time as This
by Rev. Dr. Joan Brown Campbell; Foreword by Karen Armstrong
A visionary minister speaks out on the pressing issues that face us today, offering inspiration and challenge. 6 x 9, 208 pp, HC, 978-1-59473-283-6 **$21.99**

Claiming Earth as Common Ground: The Ecological Crisis through the Lens of Faith
by Andrea Cohen-Kiener; Foreword by Rev. Sally Bingham
6 x 9, 192 pp, Quality PB, 978-1-59473-261-4 **$16.99**

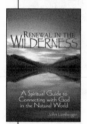

Creating a Spiritual Retirement: A Guide to the Unseen Possibilities in Our Lives
by Molly Srode 6 x 9, 208 pp, b/w photos, Quality PB, 978-1-59473-050-4 **$14.99**

Creative Aging: Rethinking Retirement and Non-Retirement in a Changing World
by Marjory Zoet Bankson 6 x 9, 160 pp, Quality PB, 978-1-59473-281-2 **$16.99**

Keeping Spiritual Balance as We Grow Older: More than 65 Creative Ways to Use Purpose, Prayer, and the Power of Spirit to Build a Meaningful Retirement
by Molly and Bernie Srode 8 x 8, 224 pp, Quality PB, 978-1-59473-042-9 **$16.99**

Honoring Motherhood: Prayers, Ceremonies & Blessings
Edited and with Introductions by Lynn L. Caruso 5 x 7¼, 272 pp, HC, 978-1-59473-239-3 **$19.99**

Journeys of Simplicity: Traveling Light with Thomas Merton, Bashō, Edward Abbey, Annie Dillard & Others *by Philip Harnden*
5 x 7¼, 144 pp, Quality PB, 978-1-59473-181-5 **$12.99**; 128 pp, HC, 978-1-893361-76-8 **$16.95**

The Losses of Our Lives: The Sacred Gifts of Renewal in Everyday Loss
by Dr. Nancy Copeland-Payton 6 x 9, 192 pp, HC, 978-1-59473-271-3 **$19.99**

Renewal in the Wilderness: A Spiritual Guide to Connecting with God in the Natural World *by John Lionberger*
6 x 9, 176 pp, b/w photos, Quality PB, 978-1-59473-219-5 **$16.99**

Soul Fire: Accessing Your Creativity
by Thomas Ryan, CSP 6 x 9, 160 pp, Quality PB, 978-1-59473-243-0 **$16.99**

A Spirituality for Brokenness: Discovering Your Deepest Self in Difficult Times
by Terry Taylor 6 x 9, 176 pp, Quality PB, 978-1-59473-229-4 **$16.99**

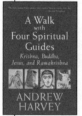

A Walk with Four Spiritual Guides: Krishna, Buddha, Jesus, and Ramakrishna
by Andrew Harvey 5½ x 8½, 192 pp, b/w photos & illus., Quality PB, 978-1-59473-138-9 **$15.99**

The Workplace and Spirituality: New Perspectives on Research and Practice
Edited by Dr. Joan Marques, Dr. Satinder Dhiman and Dr. Richard King
6 x 9, 256 pp, HC, 978-1-59473-260-7 **$29.99**

Or phone, fax, mail or e-mail to: SKYLIGHT PATHS Publishing
Sunset Farm Offices, Route 4 • P.O. Box 237 • Woodstock, Vermont 05091
Tel: (802) 457-4000 • Fax: (802) 457-4004 • www.skylightpaths.com
Credit card orders: (800) 962-4544 (8:30AM–5:30PM ET Monday–Friday)
Generous discounts on quantity orders. SATISFACTION GUARANTEED. Prices subject to change.

Inspiration

Living into Hope
A Call to Spiritual Action for Such a Time as This
by Rev. Dr. Joan Brown Campbell; Foreword by Karen Armstrong

A visionary minister speaks out on the pressing issues that face us today, offering inspiration and challenge.

6 x 9, 208 pp, HC, 978-1-59473-283-6 **$21.99**

Restoring Life's Missing Pieces
The Spiritual Power of Remembering & Reuniting with People, Places, Things & Self
by Caren Goldman

A powerful and thought-provoking look at reunions of all kinds as roads to remembering and re-membering ourselves.

6 x 9, 240 pp (est), Quality PB, 978-1-59473-295-9 **$16.99**

Bread, Body, Spirit: Finding the Sacred in Food
Edited and with Introductions by Alice Peck

Personal narratives, fiction, sacred texts and verse speak to your heart as you journey beyond physical satisfaction to the hallowed relationship between food and feeding your soul. 6 x 9, 224 pp, Quality PB, 978-1-59473-242-3 **$19.99**

Honoring Motherhood
Prayers, Ceremonies & Blessings

A spiritual voyage through blessings, prayers, anecdotes, and meditations about the sacred understanding that is motherhood.

Edited and with Introductions by Lynn L. Caruso

5 x 7¼, 272 pp, HC, 978-1-59473-239-3 **$19.99**

How Did I Get to Be 70 When I'm 35 Inside?
Spiritual Surprises of Later Life
by Linda Douty

Encourages you to focus on the inner changes of aging to help you greet your later years as the grand adventure they can be.

6 x 9, 192 pp (est), Quality PB, 978-1-59473-297-3 **$16.99**

Spiritually Healthy Divorce
Navigating Disruption with Insight & Hope
by Carolyne Call

A spiritual map to help you move through the twists and turns of divorce.

6 x 9, 224 pp, Quality PB, 978-1-59473-288-1 **$16.99**

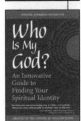

Who Is My God? 2nd Edition
An Innovative Guide to Finding Your Spiritual Identity
by the Editors at SkyLight Paths

Provides the Spiritual Identity Self-Test™ to uncover the components of your unique spirituality.

6 x 9, 160 pp, Quality PB, 978-1-59473-014-6 **$15.99**

God the *What?*
What Our Metaphors for God Reveal about Our Beliefs in God
by Carolyn Jane Bohler

Inspires you to consider a wide range of images of God in order to refine how you imagine God.

6 x 9, 192 pp, Quality PB, 978-1-59473-251-5 **$16.99**

Journeys of Simplicity
Traveling Light with Thomas Merton, Bashō, Edward Abbey, Annie Dillard & Others
by Philip Harnden

Invites you to consider a more graceful way of traveling through life. PB includes journal pages to help you get started on your own spiritual journey.

5 x 7¼, 144 pp, Quality PB, 978-1-59473-181-5 **$12.99**
5 x 7¼, 128 pp, HC, 978-1-893361-76-8 **$16.95**

Judaism / Christianity / Islam / Interfaith

Christians & Jews—Faith to Faith: Tragic History, Promising Present, Fragile Future *by Rabbi James Rudin*
A probing examination of Christian-Jewish relations that looks at the major issues facing both faith communities. 6 x 9, 288 pp, HC, 978-1-58023-432-0 **$24.99***

Getting to the Heart of Interfaith
The Eye-Opening, Hope-Filled Friendship of a Pastor, a Rabbi and a Sheikh
by Pastor Don Mackenzie, Rabbi Ted Falcon and Sheikh Jamal Rahman
Offers many insights and encouragements for individuals and groups who want to tap into the promise of interfaith dialogue. 6 x 9, 192 pp, Quality PB, 978-1-59473-263-8 **$16.99**

Hearing the Call across Traditions: Readings on Faith and Service
Edited by Adam Davis; Foreword by Eboo Patel
Explores the connections between faith, service and social justice through the prose, verse and sacred texts of the world's great faith traditions.
6 x 9, 352 pp, Quality PB, 978-1-59473-303-1 **$18.99**; HC, 978-1-59473-264-5 **$29.99**

How to Do Good & Avoid Evil: A Global Ethic from the Sources of Judaism
by Hans Küng and Rabbi Walter Homolka; Translated by Rev. Dr. John Bowden
6 x 9, 224 pp, HC, 978-1-59473-255-3 **$19.99**

Blessed Relief: What Christians Can Learn from Buddhists about Suffering
by Gordon Peerman 6 x 9, 208 pp, Quality PB, 978-1-59473-252-2 **$16.99**

The Changing Christian World: A Brief Introduction for Jews
by Rabbi Leonard A. Schoolman 5½ x 8½, 176 pp, Quality PB, 978-1-58023-344-6 **$16.99***

Christians & Jews in Dialogue: Learning in the Presence of the Other *by Mary C. Boys and Sara S. Lee; Foreword by Dorothy C. Bass* 6 x 9, 240 pp, Quality PB, 978-1-59473-254-6 **$18.99**

Disaster Spiritual Care: Practical Clergy Responses to Community, Regional and National Tragedy *Edited by Rabbi Stephen B. Roberts, BCJC, and Rev. Willard W.C. Ashley, Sr., DMin, DH*
6 x 9, 384 pp, HC, 978-1-59473-240-9 **$40.00**

InterActive Faith: The Essential Interreligious Community-Building Handbook
Edited by Rev. Bud Heckman with Rori Picker Neiss; Foreword by Rev. Dirk Ficca
6 x 9, 304 pp, Quality PB, 978-1-59473-273-7 **$16.99**; HC, 978-1-59473-237-9 **$29.99**

The Jewish Approach to God: A Brief Introduction for Christians
by Rabbi Neil Gillman, PhD 5½ x 8½, 192 pp, Quality PB, 978-1-58023-190-9 **$16.95***

The Jewish Approach to Repairing the World (Tikkun Olam): A Brief Introduction for Christians *by Rabbi Elliot N. Dorff, PhD, with Rev. Cory Willson*
5½ x 8½, 256 pp, Quality PB, 978-1-58023-349-1 **$16.99***

The Jewish Connection to Israel, the Promised Land: A Brief Introduction for Christians *by Rabbi Eugene Korn, PhD* 5½ x 8½, 192 pp, Quality PB, 978-1-58023-318-7 **$14.99***

Jewish Holidays: A Brief Introduction for Christians *by Rabbi Kerry M. Olitzky and Rabbi Daniel Judson* 5½ x 8½, 176 pp, Quality PB, 978-1-58023-302-6 **$16.99***

Jewish Ritual: A Brief Introduction for Christians
by Rabbi Kerry M. Olitzky and Rabbi Daniel Judson 5½ x 8½, 144 pp, Quality PB, 978-1-58023-210-4 **$14.99***

Jewish Spirituality: A Brief Introduction for Christians *by Rabbi Lawrence Kushner*
5½ x 8½, 112 pp, Quality PB, 978-1-58023-150-3 **$12.95***

A Jewish Understanding of the New Testament *by Rabbi Samuel Sandmel;*
New preface by Rabbi David Sandmel 5½ x 8½, 368 pp, Quality PB, 978-1-59473-048-1 **$19.99***

Modern Jews Engage the New Testament: Enhancing Jewish Well-Being in a Christian Environment *by Rabbi Michael J. Cook, PhD* 6 x 9, 416 pp, HC, 978-1-58023-313-2 **$29.99***

Talking about God: Exploring the Meaning of Religious Life with Kierkegaard, Buber, Tillich and Heschel *by Daniel F. Polish, PhD* 6 x 9, 160 pp, Quality PB, 978-1-59473-272-0 **$16.99**

We Jews and Jesus: Exploring Theological Differences for Mutual Understanding
by Rabbi Samuel Sandmel; New preface by Rabbi David Sandmel
6 x 9, 192 pp, Quality PB, 978-1-59473-208-9 **$16.99**

Who Are the *Real* Chosen People? The Meaning of Chosenness in Judaism, Christianity and Islam *by Reuven Firestone, PhD*
6 x 9, 176 pp, Quality PB, 978-1-59473-290-4 **$16.99**; HC, 978-1-59473-248-5 **$21.99**

* A book from Jewish Lights, SkyLight Paths' sister imprint

Bible Stories / Folktales

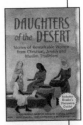

Abraham's Bind & Other Bible Tales of Trickery, Folly, Mercy and Love *by Michael J. Caduto*
New retellings of episodes in the lives of familiar biblical characters explore relevant life lessons.   6 x 9, 224 pp, HC, 978-1-59473-186-0 **$19.99**

Daughters of the Desert: Stories of Remarkable Women from Christian, Jewish and Muslim Traditions   *by Claire Rudolf Murphy,*
Meghan Nuttall Sayres, Mary Cronk Farrell, Sarah Conover and Betsy Wharton
Breathes new life into the old tales of our female ancestors in faith. Uses traditional scriptural passages as starting points, then with vivid detail fills in historical context and place. Chapters reveal the voices of Sarah, Hagar, Huldah, Esther, Salome, Mary Magdalene, Lydia, Khadija, Fatima and many more. Historical fiction ideal for readers of all ages.
5½ x 8½, 192 pp, Quality PB, 978-1-59473-106-8 **$14.99**   Inc. reader's discussion guide
HC, 978-1-893361-72-0 **$19.95**

The Triumph of Eve & Other Subversive Bible Tales
by Matt Biers-Ariel
These engaging retellings of familiar Bible stories are witty, often hilarious and always profound. They invite you to grapple with questions and issues that are often hidden in the original texts.
5½ x 8½, 192 pp, Quality PB, 978-1-59473-176-1 **$14.99**
Also available: **The Triumph of Eve Teacher's Guide**
8½ x 11, 44 pp, PB, 978-1-59473-152-5 **$8.99**

Wisdom in the Telling
Finding Inspiration and Grace in Traditional Folktales and Myths Retold
by Lorraine Hartin-Gelardi
6 x 9, 192 pp, HC, 978-1-59473-185-3 **$19.99**

Religious Etiquette / Reference

How to Be a Perfect Stranger, 5th Edition: The Essential Religious Etiquette Handbook   *Edited by Stuart M. Matlins and Arthur J. Magida*
The indispensable guidebook to help the well-meaning guest when visiting other people's religious ceremonies. A straightforward guide to the rituals and celebrations of the major religions and denominations in the United States and Canada from the perspective of an interested guest of any other faith, based on information obtained from authorities of each religion. Belongs in every living room, library and office. Covers:

African American Methodist Churches • Assemblies of God • Bahá'í Faith • Baptist • Buddhist • Christian Church (Disciples of Christ) • Christian Science (Church of Christ, Scientist) • Churches of Christ • Episcopalian and Anglican • Hindu • Islam • Jehovah's Witnesses • Jewish • Lutheran • Mennonite/Amish • Methodist • Mormon (Church of Jesus Christ of Latter-day Saints) • Native American/First Nations • Orthodox Churches • Pentecostal Church of God • Presbyterian • Quaker (Religious Society of Friends) • Reformed Church in America/Canada • Roman Catholic • Seventh-day Adventist • Sikh • Unitarian Universalist • United Church of Canada • United Church of Christ

"The things Miss Manners forgot to tell us about religion."
—*Los Angeles Times*

"Finally, for those inclined to undertake their own spiritual journeys ... tells visitors what to expect."   —*New York Times*

6 x 9, 432 pp, Quality PB, 978-1-59473-294-2 **$19.99**

The Perfect Stranger's Guide to Funerals and Grieving Practices: A Guide to Etiquette in Other People's Religious Ceremonies   *Edited by Stuart M. Matlins*
6 x 9, 240 pp, Quality PB, 978-1-893361-20-1 **$16.95**

The Perfect Stranger's Guide to Wedding Ceremonies: A Guide to Etiquette in Other People's Religious Ceremonies   *Edited by Stuart M. Matlins*
6 x 9, 208 pp, Quality PB, 978-1-893361-19-5 **$16.95**

Sacred Texts—SkyLight Illuminations Series

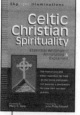

Offers today's spiritual seeker an enjoyable entry into the great classic texts of the world's spiritual traditions. Each classic is presented in an accessible translation, with facing pages of guided commentary from experts, giving you the keys you need to understand the history, context and meaning of the text.

CHRISTIANITY

Celtic Christian Spirituality: Essential Writings—Annotated & Explained
Annotation by Mary C. Earle; Foreword by John Philip Newell
Explores how the writings of this lively tradition embody the gospel.
5½ x 8½, 176 pp (est), Quality PB, 978-1-59473-302-4 **$16.99**

The End of Days: Essential Selections from Apocalyptic Texts—
Annotated & Explained *Annotation by Robert G. Clouse, PhD*
Helps you understand the complex Christian visions of the end of the world.
5½ x 8½, 224 pp, Quality PB, 978-1-59473-170-9 **$16.99**

The Hidden Gospel of Matthew: Annotated & Explained
Translation & Annotation by Ron Miller Discover the words and events that have the strongest connection to the historical Jesus.
5½ x 8½, 272 pp, Quality PB, 978-1-59473-038-2 **$16.99**

The Infancy Gospels of Jesus: Apocryphal Tales from the Childhoods of Mary and Jesus—Annotated & Explained
Translation & Annotation by Stevan Davies; Foreword by A. Edward Siecienski, PhD
A startling presentation of the early lives of Mary, Jesus and other biblical figures that will amuse and surprise you. 5½ x 8½, 176 pp, Quality PB, 978-1-59473-258-4 **$16.99**

The Lost Sayings of Jesus: Teachings from Ancient Christian, Jewish, Gnostic and Islamic Sources—Annotated & Explained
Translation & Annotation by Andrew Phillip Smith; Foreword by Stephan A. Hoeller
This collection of more than three hundred sayings depicts Jesus as a Wisdom teacher who speaks to people of all faiths as a mystic and spiritual master.
5½ x 8½, 240 pp, Quality PB, 978-1-59473-172-3 **$16.99**

Philokalia: The Eastern Christian Spiritual Texts—Selections Annotated & Explained *Annotation by Allyne Smith; Translation by G. E. H. Palmer, Phillip Sherrard and Bishop Kallistos Ware*
The first approachable introduction to the wisdom of the Philokalia, the classic text of Eastern Christian spirituality. 5½ x 8½, 240 pp, Quality PB, 978-1-59473-103-7 **$16.99**

The Sacred Writings of Paul: Selections Annotated & Explained
Translation & Annotation by Ron Miller Leads you into the exciting immediacy of Paul's teachings. 5½ x 8½, 224 pp, Quality PB, 978-1-59473-213-3 **$16.99**

Saint Augustine of Hippo: Selections from *Confessions* and Other Essential Writings—Annotated & Explained
Annotation by Joseph T. Kelley, PhD; Translation by the Augustinian Heritage Institute
Provides insight into the mind and heart of this foundational Christian figure.
5½ x 8½, 272 pp, Quality PB, 978-1-59473-282-9 **$16.99**

St. Ignatius Loyola—The Spiritual Writings: Selections Annotated & Explained *Annotation by Mark Mossa, SJ*
Draws from contemporary translations of original texts focusing on the practical mysticism of Ignatius of Loyola. 5½ x 8½, 224 pp (est), Quality PB, 978-1-59473-301-7 **$16.99**

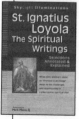

Sex Texts from the Bible: Selections Annotated & Explained
Translation & Annotation by Teresa J. Hornsby; Foreword by Amy-Jill Levine
Demystifies the Bible's ideas on gender roles, marriage, sexual orientation, virginity, lust and sexual pleasure. 5½ x 8½, 208 pp, Quality PB, 978-1-59473-217-1 **$16.99**

Sacred Texts—continued

CHRISTIANITY—continued

Spiritual Writings on Mary: Annotated & Explained
Annotation by Mary Ford-Grabowsky; Foreword by Andrew Harvey
Examines the role of Mary, the mother of Jesus, as a source of inspiration in history and in life today. 5½ x 8½, 288 pp, Quality PB, 978-1-59473-001-6 **$16.99**

The Way of a Pilgrim: The Jesus Prayer Journey—Annotated & Explained
Translation & Annotation by Gleb Pokrovsky; Foreword by Andrew Harvey
A classic of Russian Orthodox spirituality.
5½ x 8½, 160 pp, Illus., Quality PB, 978-1-893361-31-7 **$14.95**

GNOSTICISM

Gnostic Writings on the Soul: Annotated & Explained
Translation & Annotation by Andrew Phillip Smith; Foreword by Stephan A. Hoeller
Reveals the inspiring ways your soul can remember and return to its unique, divine purpose. 5½ x 8½, 144 pp, Quality PB, 978-1-59473-220-1 **$16.99**

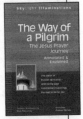

The Gospel of Philip: Annotated & Explained
Translation & Annotation by Andrew Phillip Smith; Foreword by Stevan Davies
Reveals otherwise unrecorded sayings of Jesus and fragments of Gnostic mythology.
5½ x 8½, 160 pp, Quality PB, 978-1-59473-111-2 **$16.99**

The Gospel of Thomas: Annotated & Explained
Translation & Annotation by Stevan Davies; Foreword by Andrew Harvey
Sheds new light on the origins of Christianity and portrays Jesus as a wisdom-loving sage.
5½ x 8½, 192 pp, Quality PB, 978-1-893361-45-4 **$16.99**

The Secret Book of John: The Gnostic Gospel—Annotated & Explained
Translation & Annotation by Stevan Davies The most significant and influential text of the ancient Gnostic religion. 5½ x 8½, 208 pp, Quality PB, 978-1-59473-082-5 **$16.99**

JUDAISM

The Divine Feminine in Biblical Wisdom Literature
Selections Annotated & Explained
Translation & Annotation by Rabbi Rami Shapiro; Foreword by Rev. Cynthia Bourgeault, PhD
Uses the Hebrew Bible and Wisdom literature to explain Sophia's way of wisdom and illustrate Her creative energy. 5½ x 8½, 240 pp, Quality PB, 978-1-59473-109-9 **$16.99**

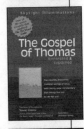

Ecclesiastes: Annotated & Explained
Translation & Annotation by Rabbi Rami Shapiro; Foreword by Rev. Barbara Cawthorne Crafton
A timeless teaching on living well amid uncertainty and insecurity.
5½ x 8½, 160 pp, Quality PB, 978-1-59473-287-4 **$16.99**

Ethics of the Sages: *Pirke Avot*—Annotated & Explained
Translation & Annotation by Rabbi Rami Shapiro Clarifies the ethical teachings of the early Rabbis. 5½ x 8½, 192 pp, Quality PB, 978-1-59473-207-2 **$16.99**

Hasidic Tales: Annotated & Explained
Translation & Annotation by Rabbi Rami Shapiro; Foreword by Andrew Harvey
Introduces the legendary tales of the impassioned Hasidic rabbis, presenting them as stories rather than as parables. 5½ x 8½, 240 pp, Quality PB, 978-1-893361-86-7 **$16.95**

The Hebrew Prophets: Selections Annotated & Explained
Translation & Annotation by Rabbi Rami Shapiro; Foreword by Rabbi Zalman M. Schachter-Shalomi
5½ x 8½, 224 pp, Quality PB, 978-1-59473-037-5 **$16.99**

Tanya, the Masterpiece of Hasidic Wisdom: Selections Annotated & Explained *Translation & Annotation by Rabbi Rami Shapiro; Foreword by Rabbi Zalman M. Schachter-Shalomi* Clarifies one of the most powerful and potentially transformative books of Jewish wisdom. 5½ x 8½, 240 pp, Quality PB, 978-1-59473-275-1 **$16.99**

Zohar: Annotated & Explained *Translation & Annotation by Daniel C. Matt; Foreword by Andrew Harvey* The canonical text of Jewish mystical tradition.
5½ x 8½, 176 pp, Quality PB, 978-1-893361-51-5 **$15.99**

Spirituality & Crafts

Beading—The Creative Spirit: Finding Your Sacred Center through the Art of Beadwork *by Rev. Wendy Ellsworth*
Invites you on a spiritual pilgrimage into the kaleidoscope world of glass and color. 7 x 9, 240 pp, 8-page color insert, 40+ b/w photos and 40 diagrams, Quality PB, 978-1-59473-267-6 **$18.99**

Contemplative Crochet: A Hands-On Guide for Interlocking Faith and Craft *by Cindy Crandall-Frazier; Foreword by Linda Skolnik*
Illuminates the spiritual lessons you can learn through crocheting.
7 x 9, 208 pp, b/w photos, Quality PB, 978-1-59473-238-6 **$16.99**

The Knitting Way: A Guide to Spiritual Self-Discovery
by Linda Skolnik and Janice MacDaniels Examines how you can explore and strengthen your spiritual life through knitting.
7 x 9, 240 pp, b/w photos, Quality PB, 978-1-59473-079-5 **$16.99**

The Painting Path: Embodying Spiritual Discovery through Yoga, Brush and Color *by Linda Novick; Foreword by Richard Segalman*
Explores the divine connection you can experience through art.
7 x 9, 208 pp, 8-page color insert, plus b/w photos, Quality PB, 978-1-59473-226-3 **$18.99**

The Quilting Path: A Guide to Spiritual Discovery through Fabric, Thread and Kabbalah *by Louise Silk*
Explores how to cultivate personal growth through quilt making.
7 x 9, 192 pp, b/w photos and illus., Quality PB, 978-1-59473-206-5 **$16.99**

The Scrapbooking Journey: A Hands-On Guide to Spiritual Discovery
by Cory Richardson-Lauve; Foreword by Stacy Julian Reveals how this craft can become a practice used to deepen and shape your life.
7 x 9, 176 pp, 8-page color insert, plus b/w photos, Quality PB, 978-1-59473-216-4 **$18.99**

The Soulwork of Clay: A Hands-On Approach to Spirituality
by Marjory Zoet Bankson; Photos by Peter Bankson
Takes you through the seven-step process of making clay into a pot, drawing parallels at each stage to the process of spiritual growth.
7 x 9, 192 pp, b/w photos, Quality PB, 978-1-59473-249-2 **$16.99**

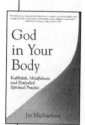

Kabbalah / Enneagram
(Books from Jewish Lights Publishing, SkyLight Paths' sister imprint)

Cast in God's Image: Discover Your Personality Type Using the Enneagram and Kabbalah *by Rabbi Howard A. Addison, PhD* 7 x 9, 176 pp, Quality PB, 978-1-58023-124-4 **$16.95**

Ehyeh: A Kabbalah for Tomorrow *by Rabbi Arthur Green, PhD*
6 x 9, 224 pp, Quality PB, 978-1-58023-213-5 **$18.99**

The Enneagram and Kabbalah, 2nd Edition: Reading Your Soul
by Rabbi Howard A. Addison, PhD 6 x 9, 192 pp, Quality PB, 978-1-58023-229-6 **$16.99**

The Gift of Kabbalah: Discovering the Secrets of Heaven, Renewing Your Life on Earth *by Tamar Frankiel, PhD* 6 x 9, 256 pp, Quality PB, 978-1-58023-141-1 **$16.95**

God in Your Body: Kabbalah, Mindfulness and Embodied Spiritual Practice
by Jay Michaelson 6 x 9, 272 pp, Quality PB, 978-1-58023-304-0 **$18.99**

Jewish Mysticism and the Spiritual Life: Classical Texts, Contemporary Reflections
Edited by Dr. Lawrence Fine, Dr. Eitan Fishbane and Rabbi Or N. Rose
6 x 9, 256 pp, HC, 978-1-58023-434-4 **$24.99**

Kabbalah: A Brief Introduction for Christians
by Tamar Frankiel, PhD 5½ x 8½, 208 pp, Quality PB, 978-1-58023-303-3 **$16.99**

Zohar: Annotated & Explained *Translation & Annotation by Daniel C. Matt; Foreword by Andrew Harvey* 5½ x 8½, 176 pp, Quality PB, 978-1-893361-51-5 **$15.99**

Spiritual Practice

Decision Making & Spiritual Discernment
The Sacred Art of Finding Your Way
by Nancy L Bieber
Presents three essential aspects of Spirit-led decision making: willingness, attentiveness and responsiveness. 5½ x 8½, 208 pp, Quality PB, 978-1-59473-289-8 **$16.99**

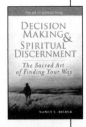

Lectio Divina—The Sacred Art
Transforming Words & Images into Heart-Centered Prayer
by Christine Valters Paintner, PhD
Expands the practice of sacred reading beyond scriptural texts and makes it accessible in contemporary life. 5½ x 8½, 192 pp (est), Quality PB, 978-1-59473-300-0 **$16.99**

Haiku—The Sacred Art: A Spiritual Practice in Three Lines
by Margaret D. McGee 5½ x 8½, 192 pp, Quality PB, 978-1-59473-269-0 **$16.99**

Dance—The Sacred Art: The Joy of Movement as a Spiritual Practice
by Cynthia Winton-Henry 5½ x 8½, 224 pp, Quality PB, 978-1-59473-268-3 **$16.99**

Spiritual Adventures in the Snow: Skiing & Snowboarding as Renewal for Your
Soul *by Dr. Marcia McFee and Rev. Karen Foster; Foreword by Paul Arthur*
5½ x 8½, 208 pp, Quality PB, 978-1-59473-270-6 **$16.99**

Divining the Body: Reclaim the Holiness of Your Physical Self *by Jan Phillips*
8 x 8, 256 pp, Quality PB, 978-1-59473-080-1 **$16.99**

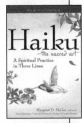

Everyday Herbs in Spiritual Life: A Guide to Many Practices
by Michael J. Caduto; Foreword by Rosemary Gladstar
7 x 9, 208 pp, 20+ b/w illus., Quality PB, 978-1-59473-174-7 **$16.99**

Giving—The Sacred Art: Creating a Lifestyle of Generosity
by Lauren Tyler Wright 5½ x 8½, 208 pp, Quality PB, 978-1-59473-224-9 **$16.99**

Hospitality—The Sacred Art: Discovering the Hidden Spiritual Power of Invitation
and Welcome *by Rev. Nanette Sawyer; Foreword by Rev. Dirk Ficca*
5½ x 8½, 208 pp, Quality PB, 978-1-59473-228-7 **$16.99**

Labyrinths from the Outside In: Walking to Spiritual Insight—A Beginner's Guide
by Donna Schaper and Carole Ann Camp
6 x 9, 208 pp, b/w illus. and photos, Quality PB, 978-1-893361-18-8 **$16.95**

Practicing the Sacred Art of Listening: A Guide to Enrich Your Relationships and
Kindle Your Spiritual Life *by Kay Lindahl* 8 x 8, 176 pp, Quality PB, 978-1-893361-85-0 **$16.95**

Recovery—The Sacred Art: The Twelve Steps as Spiritual Practice *by Rami Shapiro;*
Foreword by Joan Borysenko, PhD 5½ x 8½, 240 pp, Quality PB, 978-1-59473-259-1 **$16.99**

Running—The Sacred Art: Preparing to Practice *by Dr. Warren A. Kay; Foreword by*
Kristin Armstrong 5½ x 8½, 160 pp, Quality PB, 978-1-59473-227-0 **$16.99**

The Sacred Art of Chant: Preparing to Practice
by Ana Hernández 5½ x 8½, 192 pp, Quality PB, 978-1-59473-036-8 **$15.99**

The Sacred Art of Fasting: Preparing to Practice
by Thomas Ryan, CSP 5½ x 8½, 192 pp, Quality PB, 978-1-59473-078-8 **$15.99**

The Sacred Art of Forgiveness: Forgiving Ourselves and Others through God's Grace
by Marcia Ford 8 x 8, 176 pp, Quality PB, 978-1-59473-175-4 **$18.99**

The Sacred Art of Listening: Forty Reflections for Cultivating a Spiritual Practice
by Kay Lindahl; Illus. by Amy Schnapper 8 x 8, 160 pp, b/w illus., Quality PB, 978-1-893361-44-7 **$16.99**

The Sacred Art of Lovingkindness: Preparing to Practice
by Rabbi Rami Shapiro; Foreword by Marcia Ford 5½ x 8½, 176 pp, Quality PB, 978-1-59473-151-8 **$16.99**

Sacred Attention: A Spiritual Practice for Finding God in the Moment
by Margaret D. McGee 6 x 9, 144 pp, Quality PB, 978-1-59473-291-1 **$16.99**

Soul Fire: Accessing Your Creativity
by Thomas Ryan, CSP 6 x 9, 160 pp, Quality PB, 978-1-59473-243-0 **$16.99**

Thanking & Blessing—The Sacred Art: Spiritual Vitality through Gratefulness
by Jay Marshall, PhD; Foreword by Philip Gulley 5½ x 8½, 176 pp, Quality PB, 978-1-59473-231-7 **$16.99**

Spirituality of the Seasons

Autumn: A Spiritual Biography of the Season
Edited by Gary Schmidt and Susan M. Felch; Illus. by Mary Azarian
Rejoice in autumn as a time of preparation and reflection. Includes Wendell Berry, David James Duncan, Robert Frost, A. Bartlett Giamatti, E. B. White, P. D. James, Julian of Norwich, Garret Keizer, Tracy Kidder, Anne Lamott, May Sarton.
6 x 9, 320 pp, b/w illus., Quality PB, 978-1-59473-118-1 **$18.99**

Spring: A Spiritual Biography of the Season
Edited by Gary Schmidt and Susan M. Felch; Illus. by Mary Azarian
Explore the gentle unfurling of spring and reflect on how nature celebrates rebirth and renewal. Includes Jane Kenyon, Lucy Larcom, Harry Thurston, Nathaniel Hawthorne, Noel Perrin, Annie Dillard, Martha Ballard, Barbara Kingsolver, Dorothy Wordsworth, Donald Hall, David Brill, Lionel Basney, Isak Dinesen, Paul Laurence Dunbar. 6 x 9, 352 pp, b/w illus., Quality PB, 978-1-59473-246-1 **$18.99**

Summer: A Spiritual Biography of the Season
Edited by Gary Schmidt and Susan M. Felch; Illus. by Barry Moser
"A sumptuous banquet.... These selections lift up an exquisite wholeness found within an everyday sophistication." — ★ *Publishers Weekly* starred review
Includes Anne Lamott, Luci Shaw, Ray Bradbury, Richard Selzer, Thomas Lynch, Walt Whitman, Carl Sandburg, Sherman Alexie, Madeleine L'Engle, Jamaica Kincaid.
6 x 9, 304 pp, b/w illus., Quality PB, 978-1-59473-183-9 **$18.99**
HC, 978-1-59473-083-2 **$21.99**

Winter: A Spiritual Biography of the Season
Edited by Gary Schmidt and Susan M. Felch; Illus. by Barry Moser
"This outstanding anthology features top-flight nature and spirituality writers on the fierce, inexorable season of winter.... Remarkably lively and warm, despite the icy subject." — ★ *Publishers Weekly* starred review
Includes Will Campbell, Rachel Carson, Annie Dillard, Donald Hall, Ron Hansen, Jane Kenyon, Jamaica Kincaid, Barry Lopez, Kathleen Norris, John Updike, E. B. White.
6 x 9, 288 pp, b/w illus., Deluxe PB w/ flaps, 978-1-893361-92-8 **$18.95**
HC, 978-1-893361-53-9 **$21.95**

Spirituality / Animal Companions

Blessing the Animals: Prayers and Ceremonies to Celebrate God's Creatures, Wild and Tame *Edited and with Introductions by Lynn L. Caruso*
5¼ x 7¼, 256 pp, Quality PB, 978-1-59473-253-9 **$15.99**; HC, 978-1-59473-145-7 **$19.99**

Remembering My Pet: A Kid's Own Spiritual Workbook for When a Pet Dies
by Nechama Liss-Levinson, PhD, and Rev. Molly Phinney Baskette, MDiv; Foreword by Lynn L. Caruso
8 x 10, 48 pp, 2-color text, HC, 978-1-59473-221-8 **$16.99**

What Animals Can Teach Us about Spirituality: Inspiring Lessons from Wild and Tame Creatures *by Diana L. Guerrero* 6 x 9, 176 pp, Quality PB, 978-1-893361-84-3 **$16.95**

Spirituality—A Week Inside

Lighting the Lamp of Wisdom: A Week Inside a Yoga Ashram
by John Ittner; Foreword by Dr. David Frawley
6 x 9, 192 pp, b/w photos, Quality PB, 978-1-893361-52-2 **$15.95**

Making a Heart for God: A Week Inside a Catholic Monastery
by Dianne Aprile; Foreword by Brother Patrick Hart, OCSO
6 x 9, 224 pp, b/w photos, Quality PB, 978-1-893361-49-2 **$16.95**

Waking Up: A Week Inside a Zen Monastery
by Jack Maguire; Foreword by John Daido Loori, Roshi
6 x 9, 224 pp, b/w photos, Quality PB, 978-1-893361-55-3 **$16.95**; HC, 978-1-893361-13-3 **$21.95**

Children's Spirituality

Remembering My Grandparent: A Kid's Own Grief Workbook in the Christian Tradition *by Nechama Liss-Levinson, PhD, and Rev. Molly Phinney Baskette, MDiv* 8 x 10, 48 pp, 2-color text, HC, 978-1-59473-212-6 **$16.99** *For ages 7 & up*

Does God Ever Sleep? *by Joan Sauro, CSJ*
A charming nighttime reminder that God is always present in our lives.
10 x 8½, 32 pp, Full-color photos, Quality PB, 978-1-59473-110-5 **$8.99** *For ages 3–6*

Does God Forgive Me? *by August Gold; Full-color photos by Diane Hardy Waller*
Gently shows how God forgives all that we do if we are truly sorry.
10 x 8½, 32 pp, Full-color photos, Quality PB, 978-1-59473-142-6 **$8.99** *For ages 3–6*

God Said Amen *by Sandy Eisenberg Sasso; Full-color illus. by Avi Katz*
A warm and inspiring tale that shows us that we need only reach out to each other to find the answers to our prayers.
9 x 12, 32 pp, Full-color illus., HC, 978-1-58023-080-3 **$16.95*** *For ages 4 & up*

How Does God Listen? *by Kay Lindahl; Full-color photos by Cynthia Maloney*
How do we know when God is listening to us? Children will find the answers to these questions as they engage their senses while the story unfolds, learning how God listens in the wind, waves, clouds, hot chocolate, perfume, our tears and our laughter.
10 x 8½, 32 pp, Full-color photos, Quality PB, 978-1-59473-084-9 **$8.99** *For ages 3–6*

In God's Hands *by Lawrence Kushner and Gary Schmidt; Full-color illus. by Matthew J. Baek*
9 x 12, 32 pp, Full-color illus., HC, 978-1-58023-224-1 **$16.99*** *For ages 5 & up*

In God's Name *by Sandy Eisenberg Sasso; Full-color illus. by Phoebe Stone*
Like an ancient myth in its poetic text and vibrant illustrations, this award-winning modern fable about the search for God's name celebrates the diversity and, at the same time, the unity of all the people of the world.
9 x 12, 32 pp, Full-color illus., HC, 978-1-879045-26-2 **$16.99*** *For ages 4 & up*

Also available in Spanish: El nombre de Dios
9 x 12, 32 pp, Full-color illus., HC, 978-1-893361-63-8 **$16.95**

In Our Image: God's First Creatures
by Nancy Sohn Swartz; Full-color illus. by Melanie Hall
A playful new twist on the Genesis story—from the perspective of the animals. Celebrates the interconnectedness of nature and the harmony of all living things.
9 x 12, 32 pp, Full-color illus., HC, 978-1-879045-99-6 **$16.95*** *For ages 4 & up*

Noah's Wife: The Story of Naamah
by Sandy Eisenberg Sasso; Full-color illus. by Bethanne Andersen
Opens young readers' religious imaginations to new ideas about the well-known story of the Flood. When God tells Noah to bring the animals of the world onto the ark, God also calls on Naamah, Noah's wife, to save each plant on Earth.
9 x 12, 32 pp, Full-color illus., HC, 978-1-58023-134-3 **$16.95*** *For ages 4 & up*

Also available: Naamah: Noah's Wife (A Board Book)
by Sandy Eisenberg Sasso; Full-color illus. by Bethanne Andersen
5 x 5, 24 pp, Full-color illus., Board Book, 978-1-893361-56-0 **$7.95** *For ages 0–4*

Where Does God Live? *by August Gold and Matthew J. Perlman*
Helps children and their parents find God in the world around us with simple, practical examples children can relate to.
10 x 8½, 32 pp, Full-color photos, Quality PB, 978-1-893361-39-3 **$8.99** *For ages 3–6*

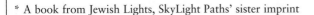

Children's Spirituality—Board Books

Adam & Eve's New Day
by Sandy Eisenberg Sasso; Full-color illus. by Joani Keller Rothenberg
A lesson in hope for every child who has worried about what comes next. Abridged from *Adam & Eve's First Sunset*.
5 x 5, 24 pp, Full-color illus., Board Book, 978-1-59473-205-8 **$7.99** *For ages 0–4*

How Did the Animals Help God?
by Nancy Sohn Swartz; Full-color illus. by Melanie Hall
God asks all of nature to offer gifts to humankind—with a promise that they will care for creation in return. Abridged from *In Our Image*.
5 x 5, 24 pp, Full-color illus., Board Book, 978-1-59473-044-3 **$7.99** *For ages 0–4*

How Does God Make Things Happen?
by Lawrence and Karen Kushner; Full-color illus. by Dawn W. Majewski
A charming invitation for young children to explore how God makes things happen in our world. Abridged from *Because Nothing Looks Like God*.
5 x 5, 24 pp, Full-color illus., Board Book, 978-1-893361-24-9 **$7.95** *For ages 0–4*

What Does God Look Like?
by Lawrence and Karen Kushner; Full-color illus. by Dawn W. Majewski
A simple way for young children to explore the ways that we "see" God. Abridged from *Because Nothing Looks Like God*.
5 x 5, 24 pp, Full-color illus., Board Book, 978-1-893361-23-2 **$7.99** *For ages 0–4*

What Is God's Name?
by Sandy Eisenberg Sasso; Full-color illus. by Phoebe Stone
Everyone and everything in the world has a name. What is God's name? Abridged from the award-winning *In God's Name*.
5 x 5, 24 pp, Full-color illus., Board Book, 978-1-893361-10-2 **$7.99** *For ages 0–4*

Where Is God? *by Lawrence and Karen Kushner; Full-color illus. by Dawn W. Majewski* A gentle way for young children to explore how God is with us every day, in every way. Abridged from *Because Nothing Looks Like God*.
5 x 5, 24 pp, Full-color illus., Board Book, 978-1-893361-17-1 **$7.99** *For ages 0–4*

What You Will See Inside ...

Fun-to-read books with vibrant full-color photos show children ages 6 and up the who, what, when, where, why and how of traditional houses of worship, liturgical celebrations and rituals of different world faiths, empowering them to respect and understand their own religious traditions—and those of their friends and neighbors.

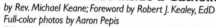

What You Will See Inside a Catholic Church
by Rev. Michael Keane; Foreword by Robert J. Kealey, EdD
Full-color photos by Aaron Pepis
8½ x 10½, 32 pp, Full-color photos, HC, 978-1-893361-54-6 **$17.95**
Also available in Spanish: **Lo que se puede ver dentro de una iglesia católica**
8½ x 10½, 32 pp, Full-color photos, HC, 978-1-893361-66-9 **$16.95**

What You Will See Inside a Hindu Temple
by Mahendra Jani, PhD, and Vandana Jani, PhD; Full-color photos by Neirah Bhargava and Vijay Dave
8½ x 10½, 32 pp, Full-color photos, HC, 978-1-59473-116-7 **$17.99**

What You Will See Inside a Mosque
by Aisha Karen Khan; Full-color photos by Aaron Pepis
8½ x 10½, 32 pp, Full-color photos, Quality PB, 978-1-59473-257-7 **$8.99**

What You Will See Inside a Synagogue
by Rabbi Lawrence A. Hoffman, PhD, and Dr. Ron Wolfson; Full-color photos by Bill Aron
8½ x 10½, 32 pp, Full-color photos, Quality PB, 978-1-59473-256-0 **$8.99**

Children's Spiritual Biography

Ten Amazing People
And How They Changed the World
by Maura D. Shaw; Foreword by Dr. Robert Coles
Full-color illus. by Stephen Marchesi

For ages 7 & up

Shows kids that spiritual people can have an exciting impact on the world around them. Kids will delight in reading about these amazing people and what they accomplished through their words and actions.

Black Elk • Dorothy Day • Malcolm X • Mahatma Gandhi • Martin Luther King, Jr. • Mother Teresa • Janusz Korczak • Desmond Tutu • Thich Nhat Hanh • Albert Schweitzer

"Best Juvenile/Young Adult Non-Fiction Book of the Year."
—*Independent Publisher*

"Will inspire adults and children alike."
—*Globe and Mail* (Toronto)

8½ x 11, 48 pp, Full-color illus., HC, 978-1-893361-47-8 **$17.95** *For ages 7 & up*

Spiritual Biographies for Young People
For Ages 7 & Up

By Maura D. Shaw; Illus. by Stephen Marchesi
6¾ x 8¾, 32 pp, Full-color and b/w illus., HC

 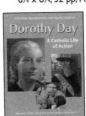 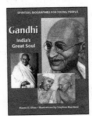 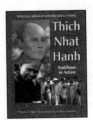

Black Elk: Native American Man of Spirit
Through historically accurate illustrations and photos, inspiring age-appropriate activities and Black Elk's own words, this colorful biography introduces children to a remarkable person who ensured that the traditions and beliefs of his people would not be forgotten.
978-1-59473-043-6 **$12.99**

Dorothy Day: A Catholic Life of Action
Introduces children to one of the most inspiring women of the twentieth century, a down-to-earth spiritual leader who saw the presence of God in every person she met. Includes practical activities, a timeline and a list of important words to know.
978-1-59473-011-5 **$12.99**

Gandhi: India's Great Soul
The only biography of Gandhi that balances a simple text with illustrations, photos and activities that encourage children and adults to talk about how to make changes happen without violence. Introduces children to important concepts of freedom, equality and justice among people of all backgrounds and religions.
978-1-893361-91-1 **$12.95**

Thich Nhat Hanh: Buddhism in Action
Warm illustrations, photos, age-appropriate activities and Thich Nhat Hanh's own poems introduce a great man to children in a way they can understand and enjoy. Includes a list of important Buddhist words to know.
978-1-893361-87-4 **$12.95**

Prayer / Meditation

Sacred Attention: A Spiritual Practice for Finding God in the Moment
by Margaret D. McGee
Framed on the Christian liturgical year, this inspiring guide explores ways to develop a practice of attention as a means of talking—and listening—to God.
6 x 9, 144 pp, Quality PB, 978-1-59473-291-1 **$16.99**

Women of Color Pray: Voices of Strength, Faith, Healing, Hope and Courage
Edited and with Introductions by Christal M. Jackson
Through these prayers, poetry, lyrics, meditations and affirmations, you will share in the strong and undeniable connection women of color share with God.
5 x 7¼, 208 pp, Quality PB, 978-1-59473-077-1 **$15.99**

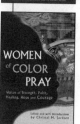

Secrets of Prayer: A Multifaith Guide to Creating Personal Prayer in Your Life   *by Nancy Corcoran, CSJ*
This compelling, multifaith guidebook offers you companionship and encouragement on the journey to a healthy prayer life. 6 x 9, 160 pp, Quality PB, 978-1-59473-215-7 **$16.99**

Prayers to an Evolutionary God
by William Cleary; Afterword by Diarmuid O'Murchu
Inspired by the spiritual and scientific teachings of Diarmuid O'Murchu and Teilhard de Chardin, reveals that religion and science can be combined to create an expanding view of the universe—an evolutionary faith.
6 x 9, 208 pp, HC, 978-1-59473-006-1 **$21.99**

The Art of Public Prayer, 2nd Edition: Not for Clergy Only
by Lawrence A. Hoffman, PhD 6 x 9, 288 pp, Quality PB, 978-1-893361-06-5 **$19.99**

A Heart of Stillness: A Complete Guide to Learning the Art of Meditation
by David A. Cooper 5½ x 8½, 272 pp, Quality PB, 978-1-893361-03-4 **$18.99**

Meditation without Gurus: A Guide to the Heart of Practice
by Clark Strand 5½ x 8½, 192 pp, Quality PB, 978-1-893361-93-5 **$16.95**

Praying with Our Hands: 21 Practices of Embodied Prayer from the World's Spiritual Traditions *by Jon M. Sweeney; Photos by Jennifer J. Wilson; Foreword by Mother Tessa Bielecki; Afterword by Taitetsu Unno, PhD*
8 x 8, 96 pp, 22 duotone photos, Quality PB, 978-1-893361-16-4 **$16.95**

Three Gates to Meditation Practice: A Personal Journey into Sufism, Buddhism, and Judaism *by David A. Cooper* 5½ x 8½, 240 pp, Quality PB, 978-1-893361-22-5 **$16.95**

Prayer / M. Basil Pennington, OCSO

Finding Grace at the Center, 3rd Edition: The Beginning of Centering Prayer   *with Thomas Keating, OCSO, and Thomas E. Clarke, SJ; Foreword by Rev. Cynthia Bourgeault, PhD* A practical guide to a simple and beautiful form of meditative prayer. 5 x 7¼, 128 pp, Quality PB, 978-1-59473-182-2 **$12.99**

The Monks of Mount Athos: A Western Monk's Extraordinary Spiritual Journey on Eastern Holy Ground *Foreword by Archimandrite Dionysios*
Explores the landscape, monastic communities and food of Athos.
6 x 9, 352 pp, Quality PB, 978-1-893361-78-2 **$18.95**

Psalms: A Spiritual Commentary *Illus. by Phillip Ratner*
Reflections on some of the most beloved passages from the Bible's most widely read book. 6 x 9, 176 pp, 24 full-page b/w illus., Quality PB, 978-1-59473-234-8 **$16.99**

The Song of Songs: A Spiritual Commentary *Illus. by Phillip Ratner*
Explore the Bible's most challenging mystical text.
6 x 9, 160 pp, 14 full-page b/w illus., Quality PB, 978-1-59473-235-5 **$16.99**
HC, 978-1-59473-004-7 **$19.99**

Women's Interest

Spiritually Healthy Divorce: Navigating Disruption with Insight & Hope
by Carolyne Call
A spiritual map to help you move through the twists and turns of divorce.
6 x 9, 224 pp, Quality PB, 978-1-59473-288-1 **$16.99**

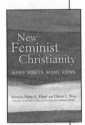

New Feminist Christianity: Many Voices, Many Views
Edited by Mary E. Hunt and Diann L. Neu
Insights from ministers and theologians, activists and leaders, artists and liturgists
who are shaping the future. Taken together, their voices offer a starting point for
building new models of religious life and worship.
6 x 9, 384 pp, HC, 978-1-59473-285-0 **$24.99**

New Jewish Feminism: Probing the Past, Forging the Future
Edited by Rabbi Elyse Goldstein; Foreword by Anita Diamant
Looks at the growth and accomplishments of Jewish feminism and what they mean
for Jewish women today and tomorrow. Features the voices of women from every
area of Jewish life, addressing the important issues that concern Jewish women.
6 x 9, 480 pp, Quality PB, 978-1-58023-448-1 **$19.99**; HC, 978-1-58023-359-0 **$24.99***

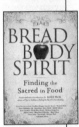

Bread, Body, Spirit: Finding the Sacred in Food
Edited and with Introductions by Alice Peck
Personal narratives, fiction, sacred texts and verse speak to your heart as you journey beyond physical satisfaction to the hallowed relationship between food and
feeding your soul. 6 x 9, 224 pp, Quality PB, 978-1-59473-242-3 **$19.99**

Dance—The Sacred Art: The Joy of Movement as a Spiritual Practice
by Cynthia Winton-Henry 5½ x 8½, 224 pp, Quality PB, 978-1-59473-268-3 **$16.99**

Daughters of the Desert: Stories of Remarkable Women from Christian, Jewish and
Muslim Traditions
by Claire Rudolf Murphy, Meghan Nuttall Sayres, Mary Cronk Farrell, Sarah Conover and Betsy Wharton
5½ x 8½, 192 pp, Illus., Quality PB, 978-1-59473-106-8 **$14.99** Inc. reader's discussion guide

The Divine Feminine in Biblical Wisdom Literature
Selections Annotated & Explained
Translation & Annotation by Rabbi Rami Shapiro; Foreword by Rev. Cynthia Bourgeault, PhD
5½ x 8½, 240 pp, Quality PB, 978-1-59473-109-9 **$16.99**

Divining the Body: Reclaim the Holiness of Your Physical Self
by Jan Phillips 8 x 8, 256 pp, Quality PB, 978-1-59473-080-1 **$16.99**

Honoring Motherhood: Prayers, Ceremonies & Blessings
Edited and with Introductions by Lynn L. Caruso
5 x 7¼, 272 pp, HC, 978-1-59473-239-3 **$19.99**

Next to Godliness: Finding the Sacred in Housekeeping
Edited by Alice Peck 6 x 9, 224 pp, Quality PB, 978-1-59473-214-0 **$19.99**

ReVisions: Seeing Torah through a Feminist Lens
by Rabbi Elyse Goldstein 5½ x 8½, 224 pp, Quality PB, 978-1-58023-117-6 **$16.95***

The Triumph of Eve & Other Subversive Bible Tales
by Matt Biers-Ariel 5½ x 8½, 192 pp, Quality PB, 978-1-59473-176-1 **$14.99**

White Fire: A Portrait of Women Spiritual Leaders in America
by Malka Drucker; Photos by Gay Block 7 x 10, 320 pp, b/w photos, HC, 978-1-893361-64-5 **$24.95**

Woman Spirit Awakening in Nature
Growing Into the Fullness of Who You Are
by Nancy Barrett Chickerneo, PhD; Foreword by Eileen Fisher
8 x 8, 224 pp, b/w illus., Quality PB, 978-1-59473-250-8 **$16.99**

Women of Color Pray: Voices of Strength, Faith, Healing, Hope and Courage
Edited and with Introductions by Christal M. Jackson
5 x 7¼, 208 pp, Quality PB, 978-1-59473-077-1 **$15.99**

The Women's Torah Commentary: New Insights from Women Rabbis on
the 54 Weekly Torah Portions *Edited by Rabbi Elyse Goldstein*
6 x 9, 496 pp, Quality PB, 978-1-58023-370-5 **$19.99**; HC, 978-1-58023-076-6 **$34.95***

* A book from Jewish Lights, SkyLight Paths' sister imprint

About SKYLIGHT PATHS Publishing

SkyLight Paths Publishing is creating a place where people of different spiritual traditions come together for challenge and inspiration, a place where we can help each other understand the mystery that lies at the heart of our existence.

Through spirituality, our religious beliefs are increasingly becoming a part of our lives—rather than *apart* from our lives. While many of us may be more interested than ever in spiritual growth, we may be less firmly planted in traditional religion. Yet, we do want to deepen our relationship to the sacred, to learn from our own as well as from other faith traditions, and to practice in new ways.

SkyLight Paths sees both believers and seekers as a community that increasingly transcends traditional boundaries of religion and denomination—people wanting to learn from each other, *walking together, finding the way*.

For your information and convenience, at the back of this book we have provided a list of other SkyLight Paths books you might find interesting and useful. They cover the following subjects:

Buddhism / Zen	Global Spiritual	Monasticism
Catholicism	Perspectives	Mysticism
Children's Books	Gnosticism	Poetry
Christianity	Hinduism /	Prayer
Comparative	Vedanta	Religious Etiquette
Religion	Inspiration	Retirement
Current Events	Islam / Sufism	Spiritual Biography
Earth-Based	Judaism	Spiritual Direction
Spirituality	Kabbalah	Spirituality
Enneagram	Meditation	Women's Interest
	Midrash Fiction	Worship

Or phone, fax, mail or e-mail to: SKYLIGHT PATHS Publishing
Sunset Farm Offices, Route 4 • P.O. Box 237 • Woodstock, Vermont 05091
Tel: (802) 457-4000 • Fax: (802) 457-4004 • www.skylightpaths.com
Credit card orders: (800) 962-4544 (8:30AM–5:30PM ET Monday–Friday)
Generous discounts on quantity orders. SATISFACTION GUARANTEED. Prices subject to change.